John

ETERNAL LOVE

Translated from Greek and Aramaic Texts

DR. BRIAN SIMMONS

BroadStreet
PUBLISHING

John: Eternal Love, The Passion Translation®
Translated from the original Greek and Aramaic texts by Dr. Brian Simmons

Published by BroadStreet Publishing Group, LLC
Racine, Wisconsin, USA
www.broadstreetpublishing.com

© 2015 The Passion Translation®

ISBN-13: 9781424549580 (paperback)
ISBN-13: 9781424549641 (e-book)

Cover and interior design by Garborg Design Works, Inc. | www.garborgdesign.com
Interior typesetting by Katherine Lloyd | www.theDESKonline.com

Printed in the United States of America

16 17 18 19 20   10 9 8 7 6 5 4 3

Translator's Introduction to John

AT A GLANCE

Author: The Apostle John

Audience: Diaspora Jews and believers.

Date: AD 80–85, though possibly 50–55.

Type of Literature: Ancient historical-biography

Major Themes: The person and work of Jesus, salvation, the Holy Spirit, and the end of the age.

Outline:

Prologue — 1:1–18
The Testimony of John the Baptist — 1:19–51
The New Order in Jesus — 2:1–4:42
Jesus as the Mediator of Life and Judgment — 4:43–5:47
Jesus as the Bread of Life — 6:1–71
Jesus as the Water and Light of Life — 7:1–8:59
Jesus as the Light and Shepherd to Humanity — 9:1–10:42
Jesus as the Resurrection and the Life — 11:1–54
Jesus as the Triumphant King — 11:55–12:50
Jesus' Ministry to His Disciples Before Death — 13:1–17:26
Jesus' Death and Resurrection — 18:1–20:31
Epilogue — 21:1–25

ABOUT JOHN

How God longs for us to know him! We discover him as we read and study his living Word. But the "Word" is not just dead letters; it's the Living Expression of God, Jesus Christ. The Word came with skin on as the Perfect Man—the One who is the divine self-expression and fullness of God's glory; He was God in the flesh!

The New Testament, at its beginning, presents four biographies to portray the four main aspects of this all-glorious Christ. The gospel of Matthew testifies that he is the King, the Christ of God according to the prophecies of the Old Testament, the One who brings the kingdom of the heavens to earth. The gospel of Mark presents him as the Love-Slave of God, the perfect servant who labors faithfully for God. Mark's account is the most simple, for a servant doesn't need a detailed record. The gospel of Luke presents a full picture of Christ as the True Man and the compassionate Savior of all who come to him. And the gospel of John unveils him as the Son of God, the very God himself, to be life to God's people.

Miracles are everywhere in the gospel of John! Water became wine. Blind eyes were blessed with sight. Even the dead rose to walk again when Jesus lived among men. Every miracle was a sign that makes us wonder about who this man truly is. The book of John brings us a heavenly perspective filled with such wonderful revelation in every verse. Nothing in the Bible can be compared to the writings of John. He was a prophet, a seer, a lover, an evangelist, an author, an apostle, and a son of thunder.

The other three gospels give us the history of Christ, but John writes to unveil the mystery of Christ. Jesus is seen as the Lamb of God, the Good Shepherd, the Kind Forgiver, the Tender Healer, the Compassionate Intercessor, and the Great I Am. Who can resist this man when he tugs on your heart to come to him? To read John's gospel is to encounter Jesus. Make this your goal as you read.

There are three things that are important to remember about John, the author of this gospel: First, he was a man who was a passionate follower of Jesus Christ. He had seen the miracles of Jesus firsthand and heard the anointed words he taught. He walked with Jesus and followed him wholeheartedly, becoming one of Christ's apostolic servants.

Secondly, John describes himself as "the disciple whom Jesus loved." This was not a term to indicate that Jesus loved John more than the others, but rather, John saw himself as one that Jesus loved. You could also say this about yourself, "I am the disciple whom Jesus loves!" Every single believer can echo John's description of himself, as those words must become the true definition of our identity.

Love unlocks mysteries. As we love Jesus, our hearts are unlocked to see more of his beauty and glory. When we stop defining ourselves by our failures, but rather as the one whom Jesus loves, then our hearts begin to open to the breathtaking discovery of the wonder of Jesus Christ.

And thirdly, it's important to keep in mind that John did not include everything that Jesus did and taught. In fact, if you put all the data of the Gospels together and condense it, we only have information covering merely a few months of Jesus' life and ministry! We are only given snapshots, portions of what he taught, and a few of the miracles he performed. From his birth to the age of twelve, we know virtually nothing about his life; and from the age of twelve until he began his public ministry at thirty, we again have almost no information given to us about him in the Gospels. John summarizes his incomplete account in the last verse of his gospel:

> Jesus did an untold number of other things than what I've included here. And if every one of his deeds were written down and described one by one, I suppose that the world itself wouldn't have enough room for the books that would have to be written.
> —John 21:25

John gives us the fourth gospel, which corresponds to the fourth of the living creatures mentioned in the book of Revelation—the flying eagle. This brings before our hearts Christ as the One who came from heaven and reveals heaven's reality to those who love him. In Daniel 3:25, it was the fourth man walking in the fire who was in the form of the Son of God. This fourth man revealed in the fourth gospel is the One who on the fourth day put the sun into the sky (Genesis 1:7).

According to one of the church fathers, Tertullian, John was plunged in burning oil in front of a massive crowd that had filled the Roman Coliseum in order to silence his ministry. But God was not yet finished with his aged apostle. Tertullian reports that he came out of the burning caldron alive and unharmed! This miracle resulted in the mass conversion to Christ of nearly all who witnessed it. John was later banished to the island of Patmos where he wrote the book of the Revelation of Jesus Christ.

This translation of John's Good News is dedicated to every faithful evangelist and preacher of the gospel. You are a gift to the world and through your ministry millions have been brought into the kingdom of God. We are forever grateful to God for your lives and your message.

You can trust every word you read from John, for he speaks the truth. His gospel will take you into a higher glory where Jesus now sits exalted at the right hand of God. As John's gospel unveils Jesus before your eyes, enter into the great magnificence of his presence and sit enthroned with him. Your life will never be the same after absorbing the glory presented to you in the book of John.

PURPOSE

The Gospel of John is all about the beautiful Christ. John tells us why he wrote this amazing book:

> Jesus went on to do many more miraculous signs in the presence of his disciples, which are not even included in this book. But all that is recorded here is so that you will fully believe that Jesus is the Anointed One, the Son of God, and that through your faith in him you will experience eternal life by the power of his name!
> —John 20:30–31

There is a two fold purpose here: he's writing to non-believers, mostly Jews but also Gentiles, to believe that Jesus is the One through whom they will find and experience eternal life; he's also writing to believers that they would more fully believe the same, to experience the fullness of that life by Jesus' powerful name.

The word believe is found 100 times in John. It is the gospel of believing! We believe that Jesus Christ is the Living Expression of God and the Light of the World. He is the Savior, the King, the true Anointed One, the Living Bread, and the Loving Shepherd. This is why we continue to teach and preach from this magisterial book: that people might have faith and grow in their faith. It is the gospel of John that reveals these truths to us.

AUTHOR AND AUDIENCE

Many believe that John penned this gospel about AD 80–85. However, the Dead Sea Scrolls hint at an earlier date as early as AD 50–55, since some of the verses found in the Dead Sea Scrolls are nearly identical to verses found in John's gospel. The earlier date, though contested by some, seems to be more likely. Why would John wait to write and share the good news of Jesus? It seems likely that John wrote his gospel prior to AD 66 when the Roman war with Jews began, for he mentions the Temple as still standing and the pool, which "has" (not "had") five porticos. All of this was destroyed during the Roman war of AD 67–70.

John was called to follow Jesus while he was mending a net, which seems to point to the focus of his ministry. John's message "mends" the hearts of men and brings healing to the Body of Christ through the revelation he brings us.

There is an interesting possibility that both James and John (sons of Zebe- dee) were actually cousins of Jesus. By comparing Matthew 27:56 to Mark 15:40, we learn that Zebedee's wife was Salome. And Salome was believed to be the younger sister of Mary, the mother of our Lord Jesus, which would make her sons, James and John, cousins of Jesus.

MAJOR THEMES

The Person of Jesus as God. Of all the major themes in John's gospel, the question of Who is Jesus? lies at its heart, especially when it comes to distinguishing it from the other three gospels. For John, Jesus is the Son of God. He does only the things that God the Father tells and shows him to say and do. Jesus is God's unique Messenger, who claims to be God and yet submits to God. Through Jesus' obedience and dependence upon him, he becomes the center for disclosing the very words and deeds of God himself. Which means the Gospel of John is as much about God as it is about Jesus!

The Work of Jesus in Salvation. John makes it clear that God the Father is the one who alone initiates human salvation. And the one who bears the Father's salvation is the Son. Jesus is the Lamb of God, come to take away the sins of the world—which means we need to be saved from those sins. He is the Good Shepherd who lays down his life for his sheep. He is also the Bread of Life, the Light of the World, the Truth, and the Life—all names that point to the salvation found in Jesus.

It is true that faith features prominently in John's gospel, calling people to make a decision and confirm it doing the truth. But John also teaches that such a decision merely reveals what God himself is doing in those who will eventually become his children—saving them through Jesus!

The Holy Spirit. The Spirit of God fills the pages of John in the way he fills the other gospels: the Spirit is given to Jesus at baptism; Jesus will baptize his people in this Spirit; Jesus is uniquely endowed with the Spirit; as the only one who has and gives the Spirit, Jesus shows us the characteristics of him. Above all, in this gospel John connects the gift of the Holy Spirit to the people of God to the death and exaltation of the Son. We have come to know the precious doctrine of the Trinity in and through much of John!

The People of God. One of the major themes of John's gospel actually draws on the Old Testament: the formation of a people, a community that will embody and carry forth Jesus' mission. This community of God's people we call the disciples begins with a sort of commissioning, where Jesus breathes upon them, marking them as his new creation people. This act recalls the original creation of the first human when God blew his breath into Adam. And like Moses' farewell address in Deuteronomy, Jesus addresses his followers (see ch. 13–17) to fulfill his redemptive purposes.

Eternal Life Now and Later. As with the other gospels, John's is oriented around the life, death, and resurrection of Jesus—the purpose of which is that humanity might have life—eternal life in the age to come, while experiencing a taste of it right now. Everlasting, unending life in this ultimate age is a gift given to people who believe in the redemption of Christ; the alternative is judgment. But this realty isn't merely for later, it's also for now; eternal life is both already and not yet. John emphasizes the present enjoyment of this eternal life and its blessings. But he also makes it plain Jesus will return to gather to himself his own to the dwelling he's prepared for them.

A WORD ABOUT THE PASSION TRANSLATION

The message of God's story is timeless; the Word of God doesn't change. But the methods by which that story is communicated should be timely; the vessels that steward God's Word can and should change.

One of those timely methods and vessels is Bible translations. Bible translations are both a gift and a problem. They give us the words God spoke through his servants, but words can become very poor containers for revelation—they leak! Over time the words change from one generation to the next. Meaning is influenced by culture, background, and a thousand other details. You can imagine how differently the Hebrew authors of the Old Testament saw the world from three thousand years ago!

There is no such thing as a truly literal translation of the Bible, for there is not an equivalent language that perfectly conveys the meaning of the biblical text except as it is understood in its original cultural and linguistic setting. Therefore, a translation can be a problem. The problem, however, is solved when we seek to transfer meaning, and not merely words, from the original text to the receptor language.

The Passion Translation seeks to re-introduce the passion and fire of the Bible to the English reader. It doesn't merely convey the original, literal meaning of words. It expresses God's passion for people and his world by translating the original, life-changing message of God's Word for modern readers.

Italicized Words and Hebrew Names

You will notice at times we've italicized certain words or phrases. These highlighted portions are not in the original Hebrew, Aramaic, and Greek manuscripts, but are implied from the context. We've made these implications explicit for the sake of narrative clarity and to better convey the meaning of God's Word. This is a common practice by mainstream translations, including the New American Standard Bible and King James Version.

We've also chosen to translate certain names in their original Hebrew or Greek form to better convey their cultural meaning and significance. For instance, it is unfortunate that translations of the Bible have substituted Miriam with Mary and Jacob with James. Both Greek and Aramaic leave the Hebrew names in their original form. Therefore this translation uses their correct cultural names, Miriam and Jacob, throughout.

———

God longs to have his Word expressed in every language in a way that would unlock the passion of his heart. Our goal is to trigger inside every English speaker an overwhelming response to the truth of the Bible. This is a heart-level translation, from the passion of God's heart to the passion of your heart.

We pray and trust this version of God's Word will kindle in you a burning, passionate desire for him and his heart, while impacting the church for years to come!

One

The Living Expression

¹In the very beginning[a] the living expression was already there.[b]
    And the "Living Expression" was with God, yet fully God.[c]
²They were together—face to face,[d] in the very beginning.[e]
³And through his creative inspiration
    this "Living Expression" made all things,[f]
    for nothing has existence apart from him!
⁴Life came into being[g] because of him,
    for his life is light for all humanity.[h]

---

a 1:1 The first eighteen verses of John are considered by most scholars to be the words of an ancient hymn or poem that was cherished by first-century believers in Christ.

b 1:1 The Greek is *Logos*, which has a rich and varied background in both Greek philosophy and Judaism. The Greeks equated *Logos* with the highest principle of cosmic order. God's Logos in the Old Testament is his powerful self-expression in creation, revelation, and redemption. In the New Testament we have this new unique view of God given to us by John, which signifies the presence of God himself in the flesh. Some have translated this rich term as "Word." It could also be translated "Message" or "Blueprint." Jesus Christ is the eternal Word, the creative Word, and the Word made visible. He is the divine self-expression of all that God is, contains, and reveals in incarnated flesh. Just as we express ourselves in words, God has perfectly expressed himself in Christ.

c 1:1 The Living Expression (Christ) had full participation in every attribute of deity held by God the Father. The Living Expression existed eternally as a separate individual but essentially the same, as one with the Father.

d 1:1 The Greek word used here and the Hebraic concept conveyed is that of being before God's face. There is no Hebrew word for *presence* (i.e. the *presence* of God), only the word *face*.

e 1:2 Both Genesis 1:1 and John 1:1–2 speak of *the beginning*. In Genesis it is the beginning of time, but John speaks of eternity past, a beginning before time existed. The Living Expression is Christ who existed eternally as part of the Trinity. He had had no beginning, being one with the Father.

f 1:3 Or "all things happened because of him and nothing happened apart from him." The Aramaic is, "Everything was in his hand (of power)." See Psalm 33:6 and Isaiah 44:24.

g 1:4 The Aramaic reads "In him was lives (plural)." Not only multiple human lives, but also spiritual life, eternal life, and life in every form.

h 1:4 As translated from the Aramaic, which can also be translated, "the spark of human life." Jesus Christ brings the light of eternal life and the full revelation of God. The gospel of John is easily divided into three sections: life (chapters 1–7), light (8–12), and love (13–21).

⁵And this Living Expression is the Light that bursts through gloom—ᵃ
   the Light that darkness could not diminish!ᵇ
⁶Then suddenly a man appeared who was sent from God,
   a messenger named John.ᶜ
⁷For he came to be a witness, to point the way to the Light of Life,
   and to help everyone believe.
⁸John was not that Light but he came to show who is.
   For he was merely a messenger to speak the truth about the Light.
⁹For the Light of Truthᵈ was about to come into the world
   and shine upon everyone.ᵉ
¹⁰He entered into the very world he created,
   yet the worldᶠ was unaware.
¹¹He came to the very people he created—ᵍ
   to those who should have recognized him,
   but they did not receive him.
¹²But those who embraced him and took hold of his nameʰ
   were given authority to become
   the children of God!
¹³He was not born by the joining of human parentsⁱ
   or from natural means,ʲ or by a man's desire,
   but he was born of God.ᵏ

---

a 1:5 Or "keeps on shining through."

b 1:5 The Greek has a double meaning here. Darkness could not *diminish* this Light, nor could it *comprehend* it. The darkness can also be a metaphor for the sons of darkness.

c 1:6 This is John, the Immerser.

d 1:9 As translated from the Aramaic. The Greek is, "the True Light."

e 1:9 Or "to enlighten everyone."

f 1:10 Or "the world (of humanity) didn't perceive it."

g 1:11 Or "to his own (things or people)."

h 1:12 Or "those who are putting faith into his name." To "lay hold of his name" means to believe all that he represents and put into practice what he taught in the power of his name.

i 1:13 Or "not from streams of blood" (i.e. the blood of a father and mother).

j 1:13 Or "from the natural realm."

k 1:13 Or "born out from God." This verse could be considered John's version of the virgin birth of Christ. The Word (message) has now "humanized" and become the messenger. However, the vast majority of translations and expositors see here not Christ's virgin birth, but the new birth of those who became "sons of God" in verse 12. Both are clearly presented in the Scriptures.

¹⁴And so the Living Expression
    became a man[a] and lived among us![b]
    And we gazed upon the splendor of his glory,[c]
    the glory of the One and Only[d]
    who came from the Father overflowing
    with tender mercy[e] and truth!
¹⁵John taught the truth about him
    when he announced to the people,
    "He's the One! *Set your hearts on him!*
    I told you he would come after me,
    even though he ranks far above me,
    for he existed before I was even born."[f]
¹⁶And now out of his fullness we are fulfilled![g]
    And from him we receive grace heaped upon more grace![h]
¹⁷Moses gave us the Law, but Jesus, the Anointed One,
    unveils truth wrapped in tender mercy.
¹⁸No one has ever gazed upon the fullness of God's splendor
    except the uniquely beloved Son, who is cherished by the Father[i]
    and held close to his heart.

---

a 1:14 Or "became visible."

b 1:14 This is the fulfillment of Isaiah 7:14. The "God with us" is Jesus Christ our Immanuel. he is *with us* in that he is in human form, a man for all eternity. The Greek and Aramaic reads, "he pitched his tent among us." This takes us back into the book of Exodus where God came down and lived in the tent (tabernacle) in the wilderness. See Exodus 25:8.

c 1:14 The Aramaic is, "We gazed upon his preciousness."

d 1:14 The Aramaic is, "Unique and Beloved Son." The Greek word, *monogenes*, means, "of a single (mono) kind (genes)." This word is also used for Isaac in Hebrews 11:17 as Abraham's uniquely precious son, but not his only one.

e 1:14 The Aramaic word, *taybootha*, means, "loving kindness or goodness." The Greek word is *charis*, which can also be translated, "grace, favor, sweetness, pleasure or delight." The translator has combined all those concepts in the words *tender mercy*. Truly, Jesus Christ is full of everything that our hearts crave.

f 1:15 This reveals the eternal nature of Jesus Christ, for John was older than Jesus. The Aramaic can be translated, "He is preferred before me, for he has priority over me."

g 1:16 As translated from the Aramaic.

h 1:16 Or "one gift after another."

i 1:18 Or "from the lap of the Father." This is an idiom for the place of closest intimacy.

Now he has unfolded to us[a] the full explanation of who God truly is!

The Ministry of John the Immerser

[19]There were some of the Jewish leaders[b] who sent an entourage of priests and temple servants[c] from Jerusalem to interrogate John. They asked him, "Who are you?"

[20]John answered them directly,[d] saying, "I am not the Messiah!"

[21]"Then who are you?" they asked. "Are you Elijah?"

"No," John replied.

So they pressed him further, "Are you the prophet Moses said was coming, the one we're expecting?"[e] "No," he replied.

[22]"Then who are you?" they demanded. "We need an answer for those who sent us. Tell us something about yourself—anything!"

[23]So, John answered them, *"I am fulfilling Isaiah's prophecy: 'I am an urgent, thundering voice shouting in the desert—clear the way and prepare your hearts for the coming of the Lord Yahweh!'"[f]*

[24]Then some members of the religious sect known as the Pharisees[g] questioned John, [25]"Why do you baptize the people since you admit you're not the Christ, Elijah, or the Prophet?"

[26-27]John answered them, "I baptize in this river, but the One who will take my place is to be more honored than I,[h] but even when he

---

a 1:18 Or "He has led the way into the knowledge of God." The Greek word, *hexegeomai*, can mean either, "to lead the way" or, "to explain."

b 1:19 Or simply, "Jews." This is a metonymy for "Jewish leaders." Obviously, not all Jews opposed John's ministry. Some estimate that John and his disciples baptized as many as one million people. It is possible that John was a part of the Essene community of devout Jews.

c 1:19 Or "Levites."

d 1:20 Or "he did not deny it."

e 1:21 See Deuteronomy 18:15. Jesus is identified as that "Prophet" in Acts 3:22.

f 1:23 As translated from the Aramaic. See Isaiah 40:3. The Aramaic is clear that the preparations are for the Lord Yahweh, signifying the deity of Jesus Christ. The Greek is, "Make straight the way for the Lord (*kurios*)."

g 1:24 Or "separated ones." They were the religious leaders of the day who considered themselves separated from sin and closer to God than other people.

h 1:26–27 As translated from the Aramaic.

stands among you, you will not recognize or embrace him! I am not worthy enough to stoop down in front of him and untie his sandals!" [28]This all took place at Bethany,[a] where John was baptizing at the place of the crossing of the Jordan River.[b]

The Lamb of God

[29]The very next day John saw Jesus coming to him to be baptized, and John cried out, "Look! There he is— God's Lamb![c] He will take away[d] the sins of the world![e] [30]I told you that a Mighty One[f] would come who is far greater than I am, because he existed long before I was born! [31]My baptism was for the preparation of his appearing to Israel, even though I've yet to experience him."

[32]Then, as John baptized Jesus he spoke these words: "I see the Spirit of God appear like a dove descending from the heavenly realm and landing upon him—and it rested upon him from that moment forward![g] [33]And even though I've yet to experience him, when I was commissioned

---

a 1:28 This was a different Bethany than the one near Jerusalem, commonly referred to in the Gospels. Some Greek manuscripts have the location as "Bethabara," however, the Aramaic is clearly Bethany.

b 1:28 As translated from the Aramaic. This place of crossing is likely where the children of Israel crossed into the Promised Land when the Jordan River parted and they passed through on dry land. See Joshua 3. This place was a powerful reminder of crossing over into a new day, a new era for Israel. This was the place chosen by God for John to baptize.

c 1:29 As the Lamb of God, Jesus was publicly washed and proven to be without flaw or blemish, ready to become the sacrifice for all the world. Although he will become the Lion of the Tribe of Judah in resurrection power, John points to him as the meek Lamb, a willing sacrifice for our sins.

d 1:29 Or "lift off (the burden)." The Greek word used here is often used for "lifting up and away" an anchor from off the ocean floor.

e 1:29 The Aramaic is, "the sins of the universe." To take away our sins is a figure of speech that means "he will break sin's grip from humanity, taking away both its guilt and power from those who believe."

f 1:30 As translated from the Aramaic.

g 1:32 Jesus, the Lamb, took away our sins, and the Holy Spirit, the Dove, brings to man the life of God. Jesus didn't come to start a movement, but to bring the fullness of life to us. This "Dove" points to the dove that Noah released from the ark. It found no place to rest in a fallen world. The last time Noah released the dove it flew and never returned. It flew throughout history over Abraham and the patriarchs, over the prophets and kings with no place to rest, until at last, there was a heavenly man who carried the life of heaven—upon him the dove (Holy Spirit) rested and remained. There was nothing that could offend heaven in the life of our Lord Jesus.

to baptize with water God spoke these words to me, 'One day you will see the Spirit descend and remain upon a man. He will be the One I have sent to baptize with the Holy Spirit.'[a] [34]And now I have seen with discernment. I can tell you for sure that this man is the Son of God."[b]

Jesus' First Followers

[35-36]The very next day John was there again with two of his disciples as Jesus was walking right past them. John, gazing upon him, pointed to Jesus and said, "Look! There's God's Lamb!" [37]And as soon as John's two disciples heard this, they immediately left John and began to follow a short distance behind Jesus.

[38]Then Jesus turned around and saw they were following him and asked, **"What do you want?"**[c] They responded, "Rabbi (which means, Master Teacher[d]), where are you staying?"[e] [39]Jesus answered, "Come and discover for yourselves." So they went with him and saw where he was staying, and since it was late in the afternoon, they spent the rest of the day with Jesus.

[40-41]One of the two disciples who heard John's words and began to follow Jesus was a man named Andrew.[f] He went and found his brother, Simon, and told him, "We have found the Anointed One!"[g] (Which is translated, the Christ.) [42]Then Andrew brought Simon to meet him.

---

a 1:33 Or "the Spirit of Holiness."

b 1:34 Some Greek manuscripts have, "the Chosen One of God." The Aramaic is clearly, "the Son of Elohim."

c 1:38 This is the first recorded saying of Jesus in the Gospels. It is a question that should be asked to every follower of Jesus: "What do you want in following me?" Do we want something only for ourselves? A ministry? Answers to prayer? Or do we simply want to be with him? Their answer, "Where are you staying?" shows that they were seeking only him. The first question God asked to Adam and Eve was, "Where are you?" The first words of the God-man were, "What do you want?"

d 1:38 The parenthetical words are added by the author, John. *Rabbi* is an honorific term that means more than teacher. The Aramaic word is best translated, "Master," or "Master Teacher."

e 1:38 Or "Where do you abide." This is the same word used in John 15:4, where it refers to life-union, to be joined to Jesus as the living vine. Jesus wants everyone to come and discover where he "abides" in life-union with his Father.

f 1:40-41 *Andrew* means "brave."

g 1:40-41 Or "Messiah." The word *messiah* is taken from the Hebrew verb, "to anoint with oil." Jesus Christ is the One anointed to deliver, to save, and to reconcile us back to God.

When Jesus gazed upon Andrew's brother, he prophesied to him, **"You are Simon and your father's name is John.**[a] **But from now on you will be called Cephas"** (which means, Peter the Rock).[b]

Jesus Calls Philip & Nathanael

[43]The next day Jesus decided to go to the region of Galilee. There he found Philip and said to him, **"Come and follow me."** [44](Now Philip, Andrew, and Peter the Rock were all from the same village of Bethsaida.)[c] [45]Then Philip went to look for his friend, Nathanael,[d] and told him, "We've found him! We've found the One we've been waiting for! It's Jesus, son of Joseph from Nazareth, the Anointed One! He's the One that Moses and the prophets prophesied would come!"

[46]Nathanael sneered, "Nazareth! What good thing could ever come from Nazareth?"[e] Philip answered, "Come and let's find out!"

[47]When Jesus saw Nathanael approaching, he said, **"Now here comes a true son of Israel—an honest man with no hidden motive!"**

[48]*Nathanael was stunned* and said, "But you've never met me—how do you know anything about me?"

Jesus answered, **"Nathanael, right before Philip came to you I saw you sitting under the shade of a fig tree."**[f]

---

a 1:42 The Aramaic can also be translated, "You are Simon, son of the Dove." Simon means, "one who hears."

b 1:42 The Aramaic word is *Keefa*, which means "rock." It is Anglicized as "Peter." This parenthetical statement is not found in the Aramaic, but only in Greek manuscripts. It appears that the Greek text is admitting it is a translation from the Aramaic.

c 1:44 Bethsaida means, "Place of Fishing," and was a village on the Sea of Galilee.

d 1:45 Nathanael means, "Gift of God." It is commonly thought that he is the same one as the Bartholomew mentioned as one of Christ's apostles. Almost every time Philip's name is listed as an apostle, it is followed by Bartholomew. The word *friend* is implied.

e 1:46 Jesus and his disciples were Galileans and spoke the northern dialect of Aramaic. Galileans were considered somewhat backward. Isaiah called that region "the land of the Gentile peoples, those surrounded with great darkness." Yet this was the region where the Messiah's light would shine forth. See Isaiah 9:1–2.

f 1:48 Although we can only speculate what Nathanael was doing while sitting under the fig tree, it had to have been something very personal to him. Perhaps he was confessing to God his love for him and his desire to be pure and holy. Or perhaps he was meditating on the Scriptures that speak of the coming Messiah. A fig tree is often a Biblical metaphor of God's purpose and destiny coming

⁴⁹Nathanael blurted out, "Teacher, you are truly the Son of God and the King of Israel!"

⁵⁰Jesus answered, **"Do you believe simply because I told you I saw you sitting under a fig tree? You will experience even more impressive things than that!** ⁵¹**I prophesy to you eternal truth:**[a] **From now on**[b] **you will see**[c] **an open heaven and gaze upon the Son of Man**[d] **like a Stairway reaching into the sky**[e] **with the messengers of God climbing up and down upon**[f] **him!"**

Two

Jesus Comes to a Wedding

¹Now on the third day[g] there was a wedding feast in the Galilean village of Cana,[h] and the mother of Jesus was there. ²⁻³Jesus and his disciples were

---

to fruitfulness, especially as it relates to God's kingdom realm being established on the earth. See Micah 4:4 and Zechariah 3:10. There is some speculation that the phrase "I saw you under the fig tree" could be an Aramaic idiom for, "I knew you since you were in the cradle."

a 1:51 As translated from the Aramaic. John records Jesus using this phrase twenty-five times. The Greek is, "Amen, Amen I say to you."

b 1:51 As translated from the Aramaic.

c 1:51 Or "you (plural) will spiritually see." This is a promise for every believer today.

d 1:51 This is a messianic term pointing to Christ, not as the son of a man, but the Son of Man (humanity). he is the True Man. He is not Joseph's son, but the Son of God.

e 1:51 This is an obvious reference to "Jacob's Ladder" as the fulfillment of his dream found in Genesis 28:10-22. Jesus Christ is that Stairway that joins earth to heaven and brings heaven to earth. The word for *angels* can be translated "messengers" and could be humans given access into the heavenly realm through the blood of Jesus. Jesus, as the Stairway, is both in heaven and on earth as he speaks this to Nathanael. What mysteries surround him!

f 1:51 Or "next to."

g 2:1 This was a Tuesday as counted by the Hebrew week beginning on Sunday. Tuesdays were ideal for Jewish weddings, for that gave the guests time to get there after the Sabbath and remain for the multiple days of the wedding feast. The third day is also a picture of the day of resurrection glory, the day Jesus rose from the dead. This miracle is a revelation of going from death to resurrection life, water to wine.

h 2:1 Cana means, "land of reeds," which points to the weak and fragile nature of man. See Isaiah

all invited to the banquet,[a] but with so many guests in attendance, they ran out of wine.[b] And when Miriam[c] realized it, she came to him and asked, "They have no wine, *can't you do something about it?"*[d]

[4]Jesus replied, **"My dear one, don't you understand that if I do this, it won't change anything for you, but it will change everything for me!**[e] My hour *of unveiling my power* has not yet come."

[5]Mary then went to the servers and told them, "Whatever Jesus tells you, make sure that you do it!"

[6]Now there were six stone water pots[f] standing nearby. They were meant to be used for the Jewish washing rituals.[g] Each one held about 20 gallons or more. [7]Jesus came to the servers and told them, **"Fill the pots with water, right up to the very brim."** [8]Then he said, **"Now fill your pitchers and take them to the master of ceremonies."**

[9]And when they poured out their pitcher for the master of ceremonies to sample, the water became wine! When he tasted the water that became

---

42:3 and Matthew 11:17 and 12:20.

a 2:2-3 There is speculation that this wedding involved someone of Jesus' family since Miriam (Mary) and all his disciples were also in attendance. A Near Eastern wedding would often last between three and seven days.

b 2:2-3 Interpreting Miriam's (Mary's) words for today we could say, "Religion has failed, it has run out of wine." The traditions of religion cannot gladden the heart, but Jesus can. Moses (the Law) turned water into blood, but Jesus (grace) turned water into wine.

c Or "Mary." It is unfortunate that translations of the Bible have substituted Miriam with Mary. Both Greek and Aramaic leave the Hebrew name as it is, Miriam. This translation will use the correct name, Miriam, throughout.

d 2:2-3 This is a dilemma that Miriam (Mary) is hoping Jesus will solve by performing a miracle. Miriam (Mary) has no doubt about the power and anointing of her Son. Running out of wine is a picture of how the joy of this world runs out and fades away.

e 2:4 Or most literally, "Woman, what is that for you and for me?" This is an Aramaic idiom meaning, "What do we have in common if I do this?" For Miriam (Mary), it will change her very little, but for Jesus, this will be his first public miracle and will dramatically change his ministry from this moment on as the crowds see the power that he possesses. Jesus knows his miracle ministry will "come out of hiding" by performing a miracle. Yet with Miriam's (Mary's) encouragement, Jesus proceeds to do just that.

f 2:6 Six is the number for man, for man was made on the sixth day. These six jars could represent man's method of helping others. It is nothing but water. But Jesus changes the water of the Word of God into the Wine of the Spirit. True spiritual life can fill our vessel as we bring joy to the world. The fruit of the Spirit is joy, and there is no limit on the joy available for the child of God. See Galatians 5:23.

g 2:6 This was an outward purification (baptism) for worshippers coming into a synagogue.

wine, the master of ceremonies was impressed. (Although he didn't know where the wine had come from, but the servers knew.) [10]He called the bridegroom over and said to him, "Every host serves his best wine first until everyone has had a cup or two, then he serves the wine of poor quality. But you, my friend, you've reserved the most exquisite wine until now!"[a]

[11]This miracle in Cana was the first of the many extraordinary miracles Jesus performed in Galilee. This was a sign revealing his glory, and his disciples believed in him.[b]

Jesus at the Temple

[12]After this, Jesus, his mother and brothers and his disciples went to Capernaum and stayed there for a few days. [13]But the time was close for the Jewish Passover to begin, so Jesus walked to Jerusalem.[c] [14]As he went into the temple courtyard, he noticed it was filled with merchants selling oxen, lambs, and doves *for exorbitant prices*, while others were overcharging as they exchanged currency[d] behind their counters. [15]So Jesus found some rope and made it into a whip. Then he drove out every one of them and their animals from the courtyard of the temple, and he kicked over their tables filled with money, scattering it everywhere![e] [16]And he shouted at the merchants,[f] **"Get these things out of here! Don't you dare make my Father's house into a center for merchandise!"** [17]That's when his disciples remembered the Scripture: "I am consumed with a fiery passion to keep your house pure!"[g]

---

a 2:10 Jesus delights in your joy more than you know. He does not withhold joy from his people. He created between 120 and 150 gallons of the very best wine for a wedding feast! This was one of five miracles that are unique to John's gospel. The other four are: healing the rich man's son (John 4), healing the crippled man at Bethesda (John 5), healing the blind man (John 9), and raising Lazarus from the dead (John 11).

b 2:11 Or "The disciples made known his glory and believed in him."

c 2:13 This was a journey of nearly eighty miles.

d 2:14 These money changers would exchange Roman currency into Jewish currency to pay the temple tax.

e 2:15 Jesus came to end animal sacrifices and to end the financial tyranny of religion.

f 2:16 Or "the dove dealers."

g 2:17 See Psalm 69:9.

¹⁸But the Jewish religious leaders challenged Jesus, "What authorization do you have to do this sort of thing? If God gave you this kind of authority, what *supernatural* sign will you show us to prove it?"

¹⁹Jesus answered, **"After you've destroyed this temple,**[a] **I will raise it up again in three days."**

²⁰Then the Jewish leaders sneered, "This temple took forty-six years[b] to build, and you mean to tell us that you will raise it up in three days?" ²¹*But they didn't understand that* Jesus was speaking of the "temple" of his body.[c] ²²But the disciples remembered his prophecy after Jesus rose from the dead, and believed both the Scripture and what Jesus had said.

²³While Jesus was at the Passover Feast, *the number of his followers began to grow*, and many gave their allegiance to him because of all the miraculous signs they had seen him doing! ²⁴But Jesus did not yet entrust himself to them, because he knew how fickle human hearts can be. ²⁵He didn't need anyone to tell him about human nature, *for he fully understood what man was capable of doing.*

Three

Nicodemus

¹Now there was a prominent religious leader among the Jews named Nicodemus,[d] who was part of the sect called the Pharisees and a member of

---

a 2:19 Or "sanctuary."

b 2:20 Our bodies (temples) have forty-six chromosomes in every cell.

c 2:21 Resurrection power would be the sign of his supreme authority. Jesus' death and resurrection effectively dismantled the need for the temple, for now his powerful gospel of the kingdom realm builds us into a holy temple not made with hands. See 1 Corinthians 3:16 and 6:19. This symbolic form of speaking was so different than the teachings of the Pharisees, as it is to the understanding of many Christians today. The God who was once worshipped by animal sacrifices is now to be worshipped in spirit and truth with every believer as a priest.

d 3:1 Nicodemus means, "Conqueror." Here we see a distinguished and moral man speaking with Jesus. In the next chapter we will see an immoral woman coming to know Jesus, the woman at Jacob's well.

the Jewish ruling council. ²One night he discreetly came to Jesus and said, "Master, we know that you are a teacher from God, for no one performs the miracle signs that you do, unless God's power is with him."

³Jesus answered, **"Nicodemus, listen to this eternal truth: Before a person can perceive God's kingdom realm, they must first experience a rebirth."**[a]

⁴Nicodemus said, "Rebirth? How can a grey-headed man be reborn? It's impossible for a man to go back into the womb a second time and be reborn!"

⁵Jesus answered, **"I speak an eternal truth: Unless you are born of water[b] and Spirit-wind, you will never enter God's kingdom realm. ⁶For the natural realm can only give birth to things that are natural, but the spiritual realm gives birth to supernatural life!**

⁷**"You shouldn't be amazed by my statement,[c] 'You must be born from above!'[d] ⁸For the spirit-wind blows as it chooses. You can hear its sound, but you don't know where it came from or where it's going. So it is within the hearts of those who are Spirit-born!"[e]**

---

a 3:3 The Greek word can be translated, "born from above." It is clear in the context that Nicodemus understood it as a rebirth. The Aramaic word is clearly, "born from the origin." The implication is that you must be born again like Adam was born by the direct breath of God. Nicodemus came seeking knowledge; Jesus offered him life.

b 3:5 This is the water of the Word of God that cleanses and gives us life. See Ephesians 5:25, 1 Peter 1:23, and James 1:18. Some see in the water and Spirit analogy the creative beginning of Genesis 1, where God's Spirit fluttered over the chaotic waters. New creation life comes the same way. It was water and blood that came from the side of our Lord Jesus. he was the last Adam giving birth to his bride from his pierced side.

c 3:7 Or "say to you all."

d 3:7 A common poetic form of Hebraic teaching is to use a play on words, which Jesus utilizes in this poetic masterpiece with multiple words containing dual meanings. The word reborn can also be translated "born from above." The word for blow can also be translated "breathe." The word sound can be translated "voice." And the same word for Spirit can also mean "wind." If our new birth is so mysterious, how much more will be the ways of living each moment by the movement of the Holy Spirit? You can then understand why Nicodemus was confused, for he took everything at face value and couldn't see a deeper meaning.

e 3:8 Or "The Spirit moves you as he chooses, and you hear his voice, but you don't know where he came from or where he goes." The Aramaic is so rich and multilayered in this passage. Perhaps it could be paraphrased as, "The wind, the breath, and the Spirit are moved by mysterious moods and their own wonderful ways. When you feel their touch and hear their voices you know they are real, but you don't understand how they flow and move over the earth. In this same mysterious way so is the way of everyone who is born by breath, wind, and Spirit."

9Then Nicodemus replied, "But I don't understand, what do you mean? How does this happen?"

10Jesus answered, **"Nicodemus, aren't you the respected teacher in Israel, and yet you don't understand this revelation? 11I speak eternal truths about things I know, things I've seen and experienced—and still you don't accept what I reveal. 12If you're unable to understand and believe what I've told you about the natural realm, what will you do when I begin to unveil the heavenly realm? 13No one has risen into the heavenly realm except the Son of Man who also exists in heaven.**[a]

God's Love for Everyone

14**"And just as Moses in the desert lifted up the brass replica of a snake on a pole *for all the people to see and be healed,*[b] so the Son of Man is ready to be lifted up, 15so that those who truly believe in him will not perish but be given eternal life. 16For this is how much God loved the world—he gave his one and only, unique Son *as a gift.*[c] So now everyone who believes in him[d] will never perish but experience everlasting life.**

17**"God did not send his Son into the world to judge and condemn the world, but to be its Savior and rescue it![e] 18So now there is no longer any condemnation for those who believe in him, but the unbeliever**

---

a 3:13 Jesus shares a mystery with Nicodemus. While he was on the earth ministering, Jesus was also in heaven in the spirit realm. Being in two places at the same time is also the privilege given to every believer. We are seated with Christ in the heavenly realm and living our earthly life to please him. This is what it means to be "in Christ." See Ephesians 2:6 and Colossians 3:1–5. In the realm of the Spirit, heaven and earth is one. Jesus is telling Nicodemus that only those who are seated in the heavenly realm will understand spiritual truths. See 1 Corinthians 2:1–10. There are some Greek manuscripts that read, "the Son of Man who came from heaven." But the Aramaic is clearly, "who is in heaven."

b 3:14 See Numbers 21:8–9. The brass snake was an emblem of sin and disease. The Hebrew uses a word, *seraph*, which means a fiery one (fiery serpent). All of humanity has been bitten by the "snake of sin," but Jesus was raised up on a cross for all the people to see on a hill. We only need to look to him and believe, and we are healed and saved from sin.

c 3:16 Or "God proved he loved the world by giving his Son."

d 3:16 Or "believe into him." Salvation and regeneration must be by faith. True faith (Gr. *pistis*) has a number of components: acceptance, embracing something (someone) as truth, union with God and his Word, and an inner confidence that God alone is enough.

e 3:17 The Aramaic is, "so that they shall live by his hand (of power)."

already lives under condemnation because they do not believe in the name of God's beloved Son.[a] [19]And here is the basis for their judgment: The Light of God has now come into the world, but the hearts of people love their darkness more than the Light, because they want the darkness to conceal their evil. [20]So the wicked[b] hate the Light and try to hide from it, for their lives are fully exposed in the Light. [21]But those who love the Truth[c] will come out into the Light and welcome its exposure, for the Light will reveal that their fruitful works were produced by God."[d]

John, Friend of the Bridegroom

[22]Then Jesus and his disciples went out for a length of time into the Judean countryside where they baptized the people. [23]At this time John was still baptizing people at Aenon,[e] near Salim,[f] where there was plenty of water. And the people kept coming for John to baptize them. [24](This was before John was thrown into prison.)

[25]An argument then developed between John's disciples and a particular Jewish man about baptism.[g] [26]So they went to John and asked him, "Teacher, are you aware that the One you told us about at the crossing place—he's now baptizing everyone with larger crowds than yours. People are flocking to him! *What do you think about that?*"

[27]John answered them, "A person cannot receive even one thing unless God bestows it.[h] [28]You heard me tell you before that I am not the

---

a 3:18 Or "One and Only Son."

b 3:20 The Aramaic is, "Those who do hateful things."

c 3:21 Or "practice the truth."

d 3:21 Some scholars believe that verses 16–21 are explanatory material supplied by John, the author, rather than the words of Jesus.

e 3:23 The Aramaic location is *Ainyon*, which in Aramaic means, "the spring of doves," or, "dove's eyes." The Greek manuscripts have transliterated this to *Aenon*.

f 3:23 Or in Aramaic, *Shalim*, which means, "to follow." One ancient tradition refers to this location to be eight miles south of the town of Scythopolis, or *Beit She'an*.

g 3:25 Or "purification." The implication is that the Jewish man was telling John's disciples that Jesus' baptism was better than John's.

h 3:27 Or "No one of his own will can receive anything unless it comes to him from heaven."

Messiah, but certainly I am the messenger sent ahead of him. [29]He is the Bridegroom,[a] and I the bride belongs to him. I am the friend[b] of the Bridegroom who stands nearby and listens with great joy to the Bridegroom's voice. And because of his words my joy is complete and overflows! [30]So it's necessary for him to increase[c] and for me to be diminished.[d]

[31]"For the one who is from the earth belongs to the earth and speaks from the natural realm. But the One who comes from above is above everything and speaks of the highest realm of all! [32]His message is about what he has seen and experienced, even though people don't accept it. [33]Yet those who embrace his message know in their hearts that it's the truth.[e]

[34]"The One whom God has sent to represent him will speak the words of God, for God has poured out upon him the fullness of the Holy Spirit without limitation.[f] [35]The Father loves his Son so much that all things have been given into his hands.[g] [36]Those who trust in the Son possess eternal life; but those who don't obey[h] the Son will not see life, and God's anger will rise up against them.[i]

---

a 3:29 See Isaiah 62:5 and Revelation 21:9.

b 3:29 Or "family member."

c 3:30 The increase of Christ in verse 30 is the bride of Christ in verse 29. We are the increase of Christ as his counterpart. Just as Eve was the increase of Adam, the bride is the increase of Christ on the earth. See Isaiah 9:6–7.

d 3:30 Or "he is destined to become greater, and I must be pruned." Some translations end John the Immerser's words here and make verses 31–36 the words of John the Apostle.

e 3:33 The Aramaic is, "Those who accept his testimony take God's true seal (upon them)."

f 3:34 Or "the Spirit does not give anything in small measures." There is some textual evidence that this verse is saying, "The Son gives the Spirit (to his people) without measure."

g 3:35 The text is simply, "he has given all into his hands." The "all" can be all things, or "all authority," but can also mean, "all people."

h 3:36 The Aramaic can be translated, "those who do not cling onto the Son."

i 3:36 As translated from the Aramaic. The Greek is, "wrath rests upon them."

Four

A Thirsty Savior

[1]Soon the news reached the Jewish religious leaders known as the Pharisees that Jesus was drawing greater crowds of followers coming to be baptized than John. [2](Although Jesus didn't baptize, but had his disciples baptize the people.) [3]Jesus[a] heard what was being said and abruptly left Judea and returned to the province of Galilee, [4]and he had to pass through Samaritan territory.

[5]Jesus arrived at the Samaritan village of Sychar,[b] near the field that Jacob had given to his son, Joseph, long ago. [6-8]Wearied by his long journey, he sat on the edge of Jacob's well.[c] He sent his disciples into the village to buy food, for it was already afternoon.

Soon a Samaritan woman came to draw water. Jesus said to her, **"Give me a drink of water."**[d]

[9]Surprised, she said, "Why would a Jewish man ask a Samaritan woman for a drink of water?

[10]Jesus replied, **"If you only knew who I am and the gift that God wants to give you—you'd ask me for a drink, and I would give to you living water."**

---

a 4:3 Some manuscripts have "The Lord." This is included here from verse 1 for the sake of the English narrative.

b 4:5 This is near modern Nablus in the northern region of the West Bank. There is a village named Askar, which was formerly known as Sychar, about one kilometer north of the well.

c 4:6–8 The well was "a spring-fed well." This becomes a picture of the Jacob-life inside of every one of us. Fed by Adam's fall, this spring has flowed through all of humanity. But Jesus sat as a "lid" to Jacob's well, sealing its polluted stream. In Christ, Jacob's clever striving has ended. A living well became a lid to Jacob's well as Jesus sat there ready to give his living water to all who would come and drink. A well sitting upon a well.

d 4:6–8 The "water" Jesus wanted was the refreshing, satisfying pleasure of her devotion. He says to each one of us, "Nothing satisfies me except you." The sinner drank of the Savior and the Savior drank of the sinner and both were satisfied. Neither ate or drank, but both were satisfied.

¹¹The woman replied, "But sir, ᵃ you don't even have a bucket and this well is very deep. So where do you find this 'living water'? ¹²Do you really think that you are greater than our ancestor Jacob who dug this well and drank from it himself, along with his children and livestock?"

¹³Jesus answered, **"If you drink from Jacob's well you'll be thirsty again and again, ¹⁴but if anyone drinks the living water I give them, they will never thirst again and will be forever satisfied! For when you drink the water I give you it becomes a gushing fountain** *of the Holy Spirit,* **springing up and flooding you with endless life!"**ᵇ

¹⁵The woman replied, "Let me drink that water so I'll never be thirsty again and won't have to come back here to draw water."

¹⁶Jesus said, **"Go get your husband and bring him back here."**

¹⁷"But I'm not married," the woman answered.

"That's true," Jesus said, ¹⁸**"for you've been married five times**ᶜ **and now you're living with a man who is not your husband. You have told the truth."**ᵈ

¹⁹The woman said, "You must be a prophet! ²⁰So tell me this: Why do our fathers worship God here on this nearby mountain,ᵉ but your people teach that Jerusalem is the place where we must worship. Which is right?"

Jesus responded, ²¹**"Believe me, dear woman, the time has come**

---

a 4:11 The woman used the Greek title *kurios* when she addressed Jesus. *Kurios* is the Greek word for "lord." However, *kurios* is not a word used for "exalted or sovereign Lord," but more like "sir."

b 4:14 The Greek verb used for "springing up" is *hallomenou*, and is never used for inanimate objects (water). It is a verb used for people (living things) and means "jumping," or "leaping up." The Septuagint translates this verb elsewhere as an activity of the Holy Spirit.

c 4:16 In a sense, every one of us has been married to our five husbands: our five senses. The six men speak of our fallen humanity, for six is the number of man who was created on the sixth day. Our heart can never be satisfied with what is on this earth; we must have the living water that comes from heaven. Christ is the seventh husband, the only One who satisfies. Christ is the real husband. See 2 Corinthians 11:2.

d 4:18 After offering her living water, Jesus first confronts her with her sin and steers her away from religious debates (the proper place to worship). Then he unveils himself to her as the true Messiah. Jesus does the same thing to everyone who comes to him.

e 4:20 This is most likely Mt. Gerizim where the Samaritans had a shrine to worship God. However, Jacob's well is located at the base of Mt. Ebal, the mountain the Levites were told to curse. See Deuteronomy 27:12–26 and Joshua 8:33. Both Gerizim and Ebal are mountains in Samaria.

when you won't worship[a] the Father on a mountain nor in Jerusalem, *but in your heart.* ²²Your people don't really know the One they worship. We Jews worship out of our experience, for it's from the Jews that salvation is made available.[b] ²³⁻²⁴From here on, worshipping the Father will not be a matter of the right place but with the right heart. For God is a Spirit,[c] and he longs to have sincere worshippers who worship and adore him in the realm of the Spirit and in truth."

²⁵The woman said, *"This is all so confusing,* but I do know that the Anointed One is coming—the true Messiah. And when he comes, he will tell us everything we need to know."

²⁶Jesus said to her, **"You don't have to wait any longer, the Anointed One is here speaking with you—I am the One you're looking for."**[d]

²⁷At that moment the disciples returned and were stunned to see Jesus speaking with the Samaritan woman. Yet none of them dared to ask him why or what they were discussing. ²⁸All at once, the woman dropped her water jar and ran off to her village and told everyone, ²⁹"Come and meet a man at the well who told me everything I've ever done![e] He could be the Anointed One we've been waiting for." ³⁰Hearing this, the people came streaming out of the village to go see Jesus.[f]

The Harvest Is Ready

³¹Then the disciples began to insist that Jesus eat some of the food they brought back from the village, saying, "Teacher, you must eat something."

---

a 4:21 The Aramaic word for worship, *seged*, means "to bow down," or "to surrender."

b 4:22 Or "the life-givers are from the Jews."

c 4:24 Or "God is breath," or, "God is wind." Jesus refers to "Spirit" more than 100 times in the four Gospels.

d 4:26 Or "I am the I Am who speaks to you."

e 4:29 No doubt, this woman was the talk of the town. Having five marriages, she was well known for what she had done. For her to say these words was an honest confession of her past. The miracle here is that the people believed her and went out to see for themselves.

f 4:29 Although unnamed in the biblical account, church tradition identifies the Samaritan woman to be Photini. An internet search of her name will yield many interesting stories about her post-conversion ministry, including her being named as an "apostle" of Jesus and her eventual martyrdom. Regardless of the validity of the extra-biblical references, she will go down in history as the first New Testament evangelist to win a city to Christ. God is faithful to use anyone to reach others when we are honest to tell others that Jesus knows everything we've ever done and still loves us.

³²But Jesus told them, **"Don't worry about me. I have eaten a meal**[a] **you don't know about."**

³³Puzzled by this, the disciples began to discuss among themselves, "Did someone already bring him food? Where did he get this meal?"

³⁴Then Jesus spoke up and said, **"My food is to be doing the will of him who sent me and bring it to completion."**

³⁵*As the crowds emerged from the village, Jesus said to his disciples,* **"Why would you say, 'The harvest is another four months away'? Look at all the people coming—now is harvest time! For their hearts are like vast fields of ripened grain—ready for a spiritual harvest.** ³⁶**And everyone who reaps these souls for eternal life will receive a reward. And those who plant spiritual seeds and those who reap the harvest will celebrate together with great joy!** ³⁷**And this confirms the saying, 'One sows the seed and another reaps the harvest.'**[b] ³⁸**I have sent you out to harvest a field that you haven't planted, where many others have labored long and hard before you. And now you are privileged to profit from their labors and reap the harvest."**

³⁹So there were many from the Samaritan village who became believers in Jesus because of the woman's testimony: "He told me everything I ever did!" ⁴⁰Then they begged Jesus to stay with them, so he stayed there for two days, ⁴¹resulting in many more coming to faith in him because of his teachings.

⁴²Then the Samaritans said to the woman, "We no longer believe just because of what you told us, but now we've heard him ourselves and are convinced that he really is the true Savior of the world!"[c]

---

a 4:32 There is a fascinating word play here in the Aramaic. The word Jesus uses isn't the common word for food, but is actually a word that means "nutrients." It is also a homonym that is more commonly translated, "kingdom." Jesus has a kingdom feast that no else knows about. He feasts upon the devotion of his bride. See Song of Songs 4:15 and 5:1. The church is truly the "woman at the well."

b 4:37 See Job 31:8 and Micah 6:15.

c 4:42 They acknowledge Jesus not just as the Messiah, but the Savior of the world, including the Samaritan people who were outcasts from Judaism. The word *Savior* in Aramaic is literally translated, "Life-Giver."

Jesus Returns to Galilee

⁴³On the third day Jesus left there and walked to the province of Galilee, *where he was raised.*ᵃ ⁴⁴Now Jesus knew that prophets are honored everywhere they go except in their own hometown. ⁴⁵Even so, as Jesus arrived in the province of Galilee, he was welcomed by the people with open arms. Many of them had been in Jerusalem during the Passover Festival and had witnessed firsthand the miracles he had performed.ᵇ

⁴⁶⁻⁴⁷Jesus entered the village of Cana of Galilee where he had transformed water into wine. And there was a governmental official in Capernaum who had a son who was very sick and dying. When he heard that Jesus had left Judea and was staying in Cana of Galilee, he decided to make the journey to Cana.ᶜ When he found Jesus he begged him, "You must come with me to Capernaum and heal my son!"

⁴⁸So Jesus said to him, **"You**ᵈ **never believe unless you see signs and wonders?"**ᵉ

⁴⁹But the man continued to plead, "You have to come with me to Capernaum before my little boy dies!"

⁵⁰Then Jesus looked him in the eyes and said, **"Go back home now. I promise you, your son will live and not die."**

The man believed in his heart the words of Jesus and set off for home. ⁵¹When he was still a distance from Capernaum, his servants met him on the road and told him the good news, "Your son is healed! He's alive!"

⁵²Overjoyed, the father asked his servants, "When did my son begin to recover?"

"Yesterday," they said, "at one in the afternoon. All at once his fever broke—and now he's well!"

---

a 4:43 See verse 44.
b 4:45 See John 2:23.
c 4:46-47 The distance from Capernaum to Cana was about twenty miles.
d 4:48 Or "you all."
e 4:48 The Samaritans believed without seeing miracles.

⁵³Then the father realized that it was at that very same hour that Jesus spoke the words to him, **"Your son will live and not die."** So from that day forward, the man and all his family and servants believed. ⁵⁴This was Jesus' second extraordinary miracle in Galilee after coming from Judea.ª

Five

The Healing at Bethesda

¹Then Jesus returned to Jerusalem to observe one of the Jewish holy days.ᵇ ²Inside the city near the Sheep Gate there isᶜ a pool called in Aramaic, The House of Loving Kindness.ᵈ And this pool is surrounded by five covered porches.ᵉ ³Hundreds of sick people were lying there on the porches—the paralyzed, the blind, and the crippled, all of them waiting for their healing. ⁴For an angel of God would periodically descend into

---

a 4:54 There is an interesting parallel in Jesus' ministry in John with Acts 1:8. Jesus began first in Jerusalem (Nicodemus - John 3), then went to Judea (John 4:1-3), then to Samaria (the Samaritan woman - John 4:4-12), and then to the people with no Jewish heritage (the healing of the nobleman's son, a Gentile - John 4:46-54).)

b 5:1 Or "feast." It is difficult to determine with certainty which of the feasts it was, Passover, Tabernacles, Pentecost, or most likely, Purim.

c 5:2 The present tense *is* here in the text indicates that when John wrote his gospel, the pool of Bethesda was still there. However, by 68-70 AD, Jerusalem had been destroyed, along with the temple, by the Roman invasion. This would indicate John's gospel has an earlier date of origin than believed. It is likely that John wrote this prior to 67 AD.

d 5:2 Or Bethesda. In Hebrew, *Beit-Hesed*, which means "House of Loving Kindness." The name of this pool is found with many variations in different manuscripts. Some have "Bethsaida," or "Bethsatha," or "Belzetha." Archaeologists have discovered a deep double pool surrounded by five porticoes located near the Sheep Gate, confirming the validity of the biblical account.

e 5:2 Or "covered walkways," or "alcoves." The sick were under the "covering" of the Law, the "five" books of the Torah. But the Law cannot heal; it wounds and brings death. Christ is the healer, the living Torah.

the pool to stir the waters, and the first one who stepped into the pool after the waters swirled would instantly be healed.[a]

[5]Now there was a man who had been disabled for thirty-eight years lying among the multitude of the sick.[b] [6]When Jesus saw him lying there, he knew that the man had been crippled for a long time. So Jesus said to him, **"Do you truly long to be healed?"**

[7]The sick man answered him, "Sir,[c] there's no way I can get healed, for I have no one who will lower me into the water when the angel comes. As soon as I try to crawl to the edge of the pool, someone else jumps in ahead of me."

[8]Then Jesus said to him, **"Stand up! Pick up your sleeping mat and you will walk!"** [9]Immediately he stood up—he was healed! So he rolled up his mat and walked again! Now this miracle took place on the Jewish Sabbath.

[10]When the Jewish leaders saw the man walking along carrying his sleeping mat,[d] they objected and said, "What are you doing carrying that? Don't you know it's the Sabbath? It's not lawful for you to carry things on the Sabbath!"

[11]He answered them, "The man who healed me told me to pick it up and walk."

[12]"What man?" they asked him. "Who was this man who ordered you to carry something on a Sabbath?" [13]But the healed man couldn't give them an answer, for he didn't yet know who it was since Jesus had already slipped away into the crowd.

---

a 5:4 The majority of manuscripts do not have verse 4, and a few Greek manuscripts do not even have verse 3. However, the absence of the data found in these verses would leave a tremendous gap in the narrative, leaving unanswered why all these sick people would have congregated at the pool of Bethesda, and making verse 7 very confusing. There remains a strong basis found in a diverse set of manuscripts, both Greek and Aramaic, to argue for the inclusion of verses 3 and 4 here.

b 5:5 Under the shelter of religion, there are the sick and lame and blind who can't be healed unless they do the work and dip themselves and walk into the pool. They are helpless and hopeless so near the Sheep Gate. But Jesus has none of the Law's requirements to put upon us for our healing, only to believe in one who is greater than angels. The man had been sick for thirty-eight years, the exact length of time Israel had wandered in the wilderness. See Deuteronomy 2:14.

c 5:7 The Greek word kurios means "lord" or "sir."

d 5:10 Or "cot," or "stretcher." The Aramaic word is "quilt" or "mat."

[14]A short time later, Jesus found the man at the temple and said to him, **"Look at you now! You're healed! Walk away from your sin**[a] **so that nothing worse will happen to you."**

[15]Then the man went to the Jewish leaders to inform them, "It was Jesus who healed me!" [16]So from that day forward the Jewish leaders began to persecute Jesus because of the things he did on the Sabbath.

Jesus Responds to the Jewish Leaders

[17]Jesus answered his critics by saying, **"Everyday my Father is at work, and I will be too!"** [18]This infuriated them and made them all the more eager to devise

a plan to kill him. For not only did he break their Sabbath rules,[b] but he called God **"My Father,"** which made him equal to God.[c]

[19]So Jesus said, **"I speak to you timeless truth. The Son is not able to do anything from himself or through my own initiative. I only do the works that I see the Father doing, for the Son does the same works as his Father.**

[20]**"Because the Father loves his Son so much, he always reveals to me everything that he is about to do. And you will all be amazed when he shows me even greater works than what you've seen so far!** [21]**For just like the Father has power to raise the dead, the Son will raise the dead and give them back their life.**

[22]**"The Father now judges no one, for he has given all the authority to judge to the Son,** [23]**so that the honor that belongs to the Father will now be shared with his Son. So if you refuse to honor the Son, you are refusing to honor the Father who sent him.**

[24]**"I speak to you an eternal truth: if you embrace my message and believe in the One who sent me, you will never face condemnation, for**

---

a 5:14 Or "Don't continue sinning any longer."

b 5:18 Jesus did not break the Sabbath, he "loosed" it (literal Aramaic). He loosed it from the bondage of tradition and man-made rules.

c 5:18 They clearly understood that Jesus was claiming God as his Father in a unique way in which no one else had him as a Father like he did.

in me, you have already passed from the realm of death into the realm of eternal life!"

Two Resurrections

²⁵"I speak to you eternal truth: Soon the dead will hear the voice of the Son of God, and those who listen will arise with life! ²⁶For the Father has given the Son the power to impart life, even as the Father imparts life. ²⁷The Father has transferred to the Son the authority to judge, because He is the Son of Man.

²⁸"So don't be amazed when I tell you these things, for there is a day coming when all who have ever died will hear my voice *calling them back to life,* ²⁹and they will come out of their graves! Those who have done what is good will experience a resurrection to eternal life. And those who have practiced evil will taste the resurrection that brings them to condemnation!

³⁰"Nothing I do is from my own initiative, for as I hear the judgment passed by my Father, I execute judgment. And my judgments will be perfect, because I can do nothing on my own, except to fulfill the desires of my Father who sent me. ³¹For if I were to make claims about myself, you would have reasons to doubt.^a ³²But there is another^b who bears witness on my behalf, and I know that what he testifies of me is true.

John the Immerser

³³"You have sent messengers to John, and what he testified about me is true. ³⁴I have no need to be validated by men, but I'm saying these things so that you will *believe* and be rescued.

³⁵"John was a blazing, burning torch,^c and for a short time you basked in his light with great joy. ³⁶But I can provide a more substantial proof of who I am that exceeds John's testimony—my miracles! These

---

a According to the Mosaic laws, a man's testimony about himself is inadmissible.

b 5:32 This is the Father (See v. 37). Some believe it to be John because of verse 33. However, Jesus states that he does not need human validation.

c 5:35 Or "a lantern of chasing flames."

works which the Father destined for me to complete—they prove that the Father has sent me! [37]And my Father himself, who gave me this mission, has also testified that I am his Son.[a] But you have never heard his voice nor seen his face, [38]nor does his Word truly live inside of you, for you refuse to believe in me or to embrace me as God's messenger.

[39]"You are busy analyzing the Scriptures, frantically poring over them in hopes of gaining eternal life. Yet everything you read points to me, [40]and you still refuse to come to me so that I can give you the life you're looking for—eternal life![b]

[41]"I do not accept the honor that comes from men, [42]for I know what kind of people you really are, and I can see that the love of God has found no home in you. [43]I have come to represent my Father, yet you refuse to embrace me in faith. But when someone comes in their own name and with their own agenda,[c] you readily accept him. [44]Of course you're unable to believe in me. For you live for the praises of others and not for the praise that comes from the only true God.

[45]"I won't be the one who accuses you before the Father. The one who will incriminate you is Moses, the very one you claim to obey, the one in whom you trust![d] [46]If you really believed what Moses has written, then you would embrace me, for Moses wrote about me! [47]But since you do not believe what he wrote, no wonder you don't believe what I say."[e]

---

a 5:37 Or "testified about me." This an obvious reference to the audible voice of God that spoke over Jesus at his baptism. For this reason and the reference to God's voice, the translator has chosen to make it explicit that it refers to the Father's testimony at Jesus' baptism. See Luke 3:21–22. The fourfold witness of Christ's glory is: Jesus himself, John the Immerser, the Father who spoke over his Son, and the miracles of Jesus.

b 5:40 There were five witnesses to Christ's authority and deity in this chapter. Jesus himself (vv. 25–27), John the Baptist (vv. 32–34), Christ's miracles (v. 36), the Father (vv. 36–38), and the Scriptures (vv. 39–40, see also Psalm 40:7).

c 5:43 Implied in the text.

d 5:45 Jesus prophesies that Moses, on the final judgment day, will be the one to accuse those who would not listen to the laws and teachings of the Torah, which point to their fulfillment in Christ.

e 5:47 Apparently this concludes Jesus' ministry in Jerusalem at this time. The text does not tell us of his return to the province of Galilee.

Six

___

Jesus Multiplies Food

[1]After this Jesus went to the other side of the Lake of Tiberias,[a] which is also known as the Lake of Galilee. [2]And a massive crowd of people followed him everywhere. They were attracted by his miracles and the healings they watched him perform. [3]Jesus went up the slope of a hill and sat down with his disciples. [4]Now it was approaching the time of the Jewish celebration of Passover, *and there were many pilgrims on their way to Jerusalem in the crowd.*

[5]As Jesus sat down, he looked out and saw the massive crowd of people scrambling up the hill, for they wanted to be near him. So he turned to Philip and said, **"Where will we buy enough food to feed all these people?"** [6]Now Jesus already knew what he was about to do, but he said this to stretch Philip's faith.

[7]Philip answered, "Well, I suppose if we were to give everyone only a snack, it would cost thousands of dollars[b] to buy enough food!"

[8]But just then, Andrew, Peter's brother, spoke up and said, [9]"Look! Here's a young person[c] with five barley loaves and two small fish . . . but how far would that go with this huge crowd?"

[10]**"Have everyone sit down,"** Jesus said to his disciples. So on the vast grassy slope, more than five thousand hungry people sat down.[d]

___

a 6:1 Or "which is also called the Lake of Tiberias." Tiberias was the largest Jewish city in the Galilee province, located on the western shore of the Lake of Galilee. This could also be translated, "Jesus went *beyond* Tiberias to the Lake of Galilee."

b 6:7 Or "two hundred pieces of silver." This equates to about eight months' wages of the average person. Philip didn't answer the question and was focused on how much money it would cost, but Jesus' question was, "Where will we buy bread?" Jesus was testing Philip to see if he would look to Jesus to supply all that was needed and not consider their limited resources.

c 6:9 The Aramaic is literally translated, "boy." However, the Greek uses a word, *paidarion*, which can also mean a girl or young woman.

d 6:10 The number five thousand would have likely been only the number of men in the crowd.

¹¹Jesus then took the barley loaves[a] and the fish and gave thanks to God. He then gave it to the disciples to distribute to the people. Miraculously, the food multiplied, with everyone eating as much as they wanted![b]

¹²When everyone was satisfied, Jesus told his disciples, **"Now go back and gather up the pieces left over so that nothing will be wasted."** ¹³The disciples filled up twelve baskets of fragments, *a basket of leftovers for each disciple.*

¹⁴All the people were astounded as they saw with their own eyes the incredible miracle Jesus had performed! They began to say among themselves, "He really is the One—the true prophet[c] we've been expecting!"

¹⁵So Jesus, knowing that they were about to take him and make him their king by force, quickly left and went up the mountainside alone.[d]

Jesus Walks on Water

¹⁶⁻¹⁷After waiting until evening for Jesus to return, the disciples went down to the lake. But as darkness fell, he still hadn't returned, so the disciples got into a boat and headed across the lake to Capernaum.[e] ¹⁸By now a strong wind[f] began to blow and was stirring up the waters. ¹⁹The disciples had rowed about halfway[g] across the lake when all of a sudden they caught sight of Jesus walking on top of the waves, coming toward them. The disciples panicked, ²⁰but Jesus called out to them, **"Don't be afraid. You know who I am."**[h]

---

a 6:11 Barley is the first crop to harvest in Israel. It is a picture of the resurrected Christ. A barley loaf becomes a picture of Christ given to us in resurrection life. He is the first fruit of resurrection life. See Leviticus 23:10 and Judges 7:13–14.

b 6:11 When tempted by the devil, Jesus refused to turn stones into bread to satisfy his own hunger. Yet here Jesus multiplies bread to satisfy the hunger of others. Philip was hoping to give each one a little to eat, but Jesus' supply is always abundant, to satisfy the hunger of all.

c 6:14 See Deuteronomy 18:15–19.

d 6:15 Jesus knew the time of liberating Israel had not yet come. Men don't just need better government; we need new hearts.

e 6:16–17 Capernaum means, "the village of Nahum." Nahum means, "comfort." Or "the village of comfort."

f 6:18 Or "the Spirit stirred up on their behalf."

g 6:18 Or "three or four miles." The lake was approximately seven miles across, so they would have rowed about halfway.

h 6:20, Or "Fear not. I Am!"

²¹They were relieved to take him in, and the moment Jesus stepped into the boat, they were instantly transported to the other side!

Jesus, the Living Bread

²²⁻²³The next morning, the crowds were still on the opposite shore of the lake, near the place where they had eaten the bread he had multiplied after he had given thanks to God.ᵃ Yet Jesus was nowhere to be found. They realized that only one boat had been there and that Jesus' hadn't boarded, and they concluded that his disciples had left him behind. ²⁴So when the people saw on the shoreline a number of small boats from Tiberias and realized Jesus and the disciples weren't there, they got into the boats and went to Capernaum to search for him.

²⁵When they finally found him, they asked him, "Teacher, how did you get here?"

²⁶Jesus replied, **"Let me make this very clear,ᵇ you came looking for me because I fed you by a miracle, not because you believe in me. ²⁷Why would you strive for food that is perishable and not be passionate to seek the food of eternal life, which never spoils?ᶜ I, the Son of Man, am ready to give you what matters most, for God the Father has destined me for this purpose."ᵈ**

²⁸They replied, "So what should we do if we want to do God's work?"

²⁹Jesus answered, **"The work you can do for God starts with believing in the One he has sent."**

³⁰⁻³¹They replied, "Show us a miracle so we can see it, and then we'll believe in you. *Moses took care of our ancestors* who were fed by the miracle of mannaᵉ every day in the desert, just like the Scripture says, 'He fed them with bread from heaven.'ᶠ What sign will you perform for us?"

---

a 6:22–23 This information from verse 24 is included here for the sake of the English narrative.

b 6:26 Or "Amen, amen, I say unto you," or, "Timeless truth I speak unto you."

c 6:27 The Aramaic is, "Why would you not seek the food that fastens you to eternal life?"

d 6:27 Or "has set his seal (of approval) upon me," or, "The Father has sealed me as God with his seal of approval." The Aramaic word for "seal" can also mean "destine," or "determine."

e 6:30–31 Manna means, "What is it?" This is the bread of mystery that became the wilderness food for the Hebrews for more than thirty-eight years.

f 6:30–31 See Exodus 16:4–36, Nehemiah 9:15, and Psalm 78:24.

³²"The truth is,"ᵃ Jesus said, "Moses didn't give you the bread of heaven.

It's my Father who offers bread that comes as a dramatic signᵇ from heaven. ³³The bread of God is the One who came out of heaven to give his life to feed the world."

³⁴"Then please, sir, give us this bread every day," they replied.

³⁵Jesus said to them, "I am the Bread of Life.ᶜ Come every day to me and you will never be hungry. Believe in me and you will never be thirsty. ³⁶Yet I've told you that even though you've seen me, you still don't believe in me. ³⁷But everyone my Father has given to me, they will come. And all who come to me, I will embrace and will never turn them away. ³⁸And I have come out of heaven not for my own desires, but for the satisfactionᵈ of my Father who sent me. ³⁹My Father who sent me has determined that I will not lose even one of those he has given to me, and I will raise them up in the last day. ⁴⁰For the longing of my Father is that everyone who embraces the Sonᵉ and believes in him will experience eternal life and I will raise them up in the last day!"

⁴¹When the Jews who were hostile to Jesus heard him say, "I am the bread that came down from heaven," they immediately began to complain, ⁴²"How can he say these things about himself? We know him, and we know his parents. How dare he say, 'I have come down from heaven?'"

⁴³Jesus responded, "Stop your grumbling! ⁴⁴The only way people come to me is by the Father who sent me—he pullsᶠ on their hearts to embrace me. And those who are drawn to me, I will certainly raise them up in the last day."

---

a 6:32 The Aramaic is, "Timeless truth I speak unto you."

b The Aramaic can be translated, "a rainbow sign." Just as Noah was given a rainbow sign of the covenant God was making with him, Jesus' earthly life was a rainbow sign from heaven of the new covenant life given to every believer today. See Genesis 9 and Revelation 4:3 and 10:1. The Greek is, "true bread out of heaven."

c 6:35 The Aramaic can be translated, "I am the living God, the Bread of Life."

d 6:38 As translated from the Aramaic.

e 6:40 Or "sees the Son."

f 6:44 The Greek word is "drag," or "pull by force." The name *Moses* means "pulled (from the Nile)." The Aramaic is "ransom," or "save."

⁴⁵Jesus continued, "It has been written by the prophets, 'They will all be taught by God himself.'ᵃ If you are really listening to the Father and learning directly from him, you will come to me. ⁴⁶For I am the only One who has come from the Father's side, and I have seen the Father!

⁴⁷"I speak to you living truth: Unite your heart to me and believe—and you will experience eternal life! ⁴⁸I am the true Bread of Life.ᵇ ⁴⁹Your ancestors ate manna in the desert and died. ⁵⁰But standing here before you is the True Bread that comes out of heaven, and when you eat this Bread you will never die. ⁵¹I alone am this Living Bread that has come to you from heaven. Eat this Bread and you will live forever. The Living Bread I give you is my body, which I will offer as a sacrifice so that all may live."

⁵²These words of Jesus sparked an angry outburst among the Jews. They protested, saying, "Does this man expect us to eat his body?"

⁵³Jesus replied to them, "Listen to this eternal truth: Unless you eat the body of the Son of Man and drink his blood, you will not have eternal life. ⁵⁴Eternal life comes to the one who eats my bodyᶜ and drinks my blood, and I will raise him up in the last day. ⁵⁵For my body is real food for your spirit and my blood is real drink. ⁵⁶The one who eats my body and drinks my blood lives in me and I live in him.ᵈ ⁵⁷The Father of Life sent me, and he is my life. In the same way, the one who feeds upon me, I will become his life. ⁵⁸I am not like the bread your ancestors ate and later died. I am the Living Bread that comes from heaven. Eat this Bread and you will live forever!"

⁵⁹Jesus preached this sermon in the synagogue in Capernaum.

---

a 6:45 See Isaiah 54:13 and Jeremiah 31:34.

b 6:48 Although not found in the Greek text, there are some Aramaic manuscripts that have, "I am the living God, the Bread of Life."

c 6:54 To eat his flesh is to take into our life by faith all that Jesus did for us by giving his body for us. To drink his blood is to take by faith all that the blood of Jesus has purchased for us. This "eating" and "drinking" is receiving the life, power, and virtue of all that Jesus is to replace all that we were in Adam. Jesus' blood and body is the Tree of Life, which is offered to everyone who follows him.

d 6:56 The Aramaic is, "He that eats my body and drinks my blood is strengthened in me and I in him."

Many Disciples Became Offended

⁶⁰And when many of Jesus' followers heard these things, it caused a stir. "That's disgusting!" they said. "How could anybody accept it?"ᵃ

⁶¹Without anyone telling him, Jesus knew they were outraged and told them, **"Are you offended over my teaching? ⁶²What will you do when you see the Son of Man ascending** *into the realm* **from where he came?**ᵇ

⁶³**"The Holy Spirit is the one who gives life, that which is of the natural realm**ᶜ **is of no help." The words I speak to you are Spirit-breathed and life-giving. But there are still some of you who won't believe."** ⁶⁴In fact, Jesus already knew from the beginning who the skeptics were and who his traitor would be.

⁶⁵He went on to say, **"This is why I told you that no one embraces me unless the Father has given you to me."**

Peter's Confession of Faith

⁶⁶And so from that time on many of the disciples turned their backs on Jesus and refused to be associated with him.ᵈ ⁶⁷So Jesus said to his twelve, **"And you—do you also want to leave?"** ⁶⁸Peter the Rock spoke up and said, "But Lord, where would we go? No one but you gives us the revelation of eternal life. ⁶⁹We're fully convinced that you are the Anointed One, the Son of the Living God,ᵉ and we believe in you!"

⁷⁰Then Jesus *shocked them* with these words: **"I have hand-picked**

---

a 6:60 Jesus knows that these words were offending the religious Jews. To eat flesh that was not kosher was a violation of the law; how much more so to eat human flesh. Drinking blood of any kind was also forbidden (Leviticus 17:11). The imagery is similar to Ezekiel, who "ate the scroll" (of the Word, Ezekiel 3:1–15).

b 6:62 The greatest offense of all will be the cross where Jesus will soon be crucified, and they will watch him surrender his Spirit to the Father in death. See Galatians 5:11 and 1 Corinthians 1:18–25.

c 6:63 The Aramaic is, "the body."

d 6:66 Jesus went from feeding 5,000 to offending 5,000. They wanted him to feed them, but didn't want Jesus alone to be their feast.

e 6:69 As translated from the Aramaic. Although many Greek scholars believe this is borrowed from the Synoptic gospels, and is found in variant forms in Greek texts, the Aramaic and many Greek manuscripts have, "You are the Christ, the Son of the living God."

you to be my twelve, knowing that one of you is the devil."[a] [71]Jesus was referring to Judas Iscariot,[b] son of Simon, for he knew that Judas, one of his chosen disciples, was getting ready to betray him.

Seven

Jesus at the Feast of Tabernacles

[1]After this Jesus traveled extensively throughout the province of Galilee, but he avoided the province of Judea, for he knew the Jewish leaders in Jerusalem were plotting to have him killed. [2]Now the annual Feast of Tabernacles[c] was approaching. [3]So Jesus' brothers[d] came to advise him, saying, "Why don't you leave the countryside villages and go to Judea where the crowds are,[e] then everyone can see your miracles? [4]No one can see what you're doing here in the backwoods of Galilee. How do you expect to be successful and famous if you do all these things in secret? Now is your time—go to Jerusalem, come out of hiding, and show the world who you are!" [5]His brothers were pushing him, even though they didn't yet believe in him as the Savior.[f]

a 6:70 The Greek word for "devil" means "slanderer," or "adversary."
b 6:71 Judas is the name Judah. "Iscariot" was not his last name. There are two possibilities for the meaning of Iscariot. Some believe it is taken from a Hebrew word that means, "lock." Judah the "locksmith." He most likely was the one who locked the collection bag, which means he had the key and could pilfer the fund at will. It's his sad history that he wanted to lock up Jesus and control him for his own ends. Other scholars see the possibility that Iscariot is actually "Ish" (man) of "Kerioth" (a town once situated south of Hebron). This would mean Judas was the only non-Galilean among the Twelve.
c 7:2 Or "Tents." See Deuteronomy 16:13.
d 7:3 These were actually Jesus' half-brothers, for Joseph was his stepfather.
e 7:3 Or "so that your followers can see your miracles."
f 7:5 As translated from the Aramaic and implied in the Greek text. This fulfills the prophecy of Psalm 69:8–9.

⁶Jesus responded, **"My time of being unveiled hasn't yet come, but any time is a suitable opportunity for you** *to gain man's approval.* ⁷**The world can't hate you, but it does me, for I am exposing their evil deeds.** ⁸**You can go ahead and celebrate the feast without me—my appointed time has not yet come."**

⁹⁻¹⁰Jesus lingered in Galilee until his brothers had left for the feast in Jerusalem. Then later, Jesus took a back road and went into Jerusalem in secret. ¹¹During the feast, the Jewish leaders kept looking for Jesus and asking around, "Where is he? Have you seen him?"

¹²A controversy was brewing among the people, with so many differing opinions about Jesus. Some were saying, "He's a good man!" While others weren't convinced and insisted, saying, "He's just a demagogue."ᵃ ¹³Yet no one was bold enough to speak out publicly on Jesus' behalf for fear of the Jewish leaders.

¹⁴Not until the feast was half over did Jesus finally appear in the temple courts and begin to teach. ¹⁵The Jewish leaders were astonished by what he taught and said, "How did this man acquire such knowledge? He wasn't trained in our schools—who taught him?"

¹⁶So Jesus responded, **"I don't teach my own ideas,ᵇ but the truth revealed to me by the One who sent me. ¹⁷If you want to test my teachings and discover where I received them, first be passionate to do God's will,ᶜ and then you will be able to discern if my teachings are from the heart of God or from my own opinions. ¹⁸Charlatans praise themselves and seek honor from men, but my Father sent me to speak truth on his behalf. And I have no false motive, because I seek only the glory of God. ¹⁹Moses has given you the Law, but not one of you is faithful to keep it. So if you are all law-breakers, why then would you seek to kill me?"**

²⁰Then some in the crowd shouted out, "You must be out of your mind!ᵈ Who's trying to kill you?"

---

a 7:12 Or "He leads the people astray."

b 7:16 Or "My doctrine is not my own."

c 7:17 The Aramaic is very poetic, "Whoever is satisfied to do God's satisfaction shall gain liberating knowledge."

d 7:20 Or "Are you demon possessed?" This is an Aramaic figure of speech for lunacy.

²¹Jesus replied, **"I only had to do one miracle,ᵃ and all of you marvel!** ²²**Yet isn't it true that Moses and your forefathersᵇ ordered you to circumcise your sons even if the eighth day fell on a Sabbath?ᶜ** ²³**So if you cut away part of a man on the Sabbath and that doesn't break the Jewish law,ᵈ why then would you be indignant with me for making a man completely healed on the Sabbath?** ²⁴**Stop judging based on the superficial.ᵉ First you must** *embrace the standards of mercyᶠ* **and truth."**

²⁵Then some of the residents of Jerusalem spoke up and said, "Isn't this the one they're trying to kill? ²⁶So why is he here speaking publicly and not one of the Jewish leaders is doing anything about it? Are they starting to think that he's the Anointed One? ²⁷But how could he be, since we know this man is from Galilee, but no one will know where the true Messiah comes from, he'll just appear out of nowhere."ᵍ

²⁸Knowing all of this, Jesus one day preached *boldly* in the temple courts, **"So, you think you know me and where I come from? But you don't know the One who sent me—the Father who is always faithful.ʰ I have not come simply on my own initiative.** ²⁹**The Father has sent me here, and I know all about him, for I have come from his presence."ⁱ**

³⁰His words caused many to want to arrest him, but no man was able to lay a hand on him, for it wasn't yet his appointed time. ³¹And there were many people who thought he might be the Messiah. They said,

---

a 7:21 Or "one deed." Although Jesus performed many miracles, it is likely he is referring to the miracle of the lame man being healed in John 5.

b 7:21 This is the patriarchs. Circumcision actually began with a sign of the covenant God instituted with Abraham. See Genesis 17.

c 7:22 A son was to be circumcised eight days after he was born. See Philippians 3:5.

d 7:22 Or "Torah." Jesus is saying, "Who are you to judge me when you don't practice what you preach?"

e 7:24 Or "Never judge as a hypocrite wearing a mask."

f 7:24 Jesus is teaching that the law of mercy (healing the lame man) overrides the laws of Moses (regulations of the Sabbath). Seeing situations and people with the lens of mercy gives us true discernment.

g 7:27 This was a Rabbinical interpretation that was common in that day. However, they knew that the Messiah would come from Bethlehem, for it was prophesied in Micah 5:2 where the Christ would be born. So in truth, they did not know where Jesus was from.

h 7:28 Or "truthful."

i 7:29 Or "I am from next to him." The Aramaic is, "from his presence I Am."

"After all, when the Anointed One appears, could he possibly do more signs and wonders than this man has done?"

[32]So when the Pharisees[a] heard these rumors circulating about Jesus, they went with the leading priests and the temple guards to arrest him.

[33]Then Jesus said, **"My days to be with you are numbered. Then I will return to the One who sent me. [34]And you will search for me and not be able to find me. For where I Am,[b] you cannot come."[c]**

[35]When the Jewish leaders heard this, they discussed among themselves, "Where could he possibly go that we won't be able to find him? Is he going to minister in a different land where our people live scattered among the nations? Is he going to teach those who are not Jews?[d] [36]What did he really mean by his statement, 'You will search for me and won't be able to find me. And where I am you can't come'?"

Rivers of Living Water

[37]Then on the most important day of the feast, the last day,[e] Jesus stood and shouted out to the crowds—**"All you thirsty ones, come to me! Come to me and drink! [38]Believe in me, so that rivers of living water will burst out from within you; flowing[f] from your innermost being, just like the Scripture says!"[g]**

[39]Jesus was prophesying about the Holy Spirit that believers were being prepared to receive.[h] But the Holy Spirit had not yet been poured

---

a 7:32 Or "separated ones."

b 7:34 In this tremendous statement, Jesus is telling them that he is about to return to the realm where I Am dwells. Of course, the Jewish leaders didn't understand the impact of what he was telling them.

c 7:34 Jesus was speaking of his approaching death on the cross, which he knew was near, and his ascension back to the Father, the realm of I Am.

d 7:35 There were many of the tribes of Israel who were scattered at that time in Assyria, Iran, Afghanistan, and other adjacent nations. These had been taken captive by the kings of Assyria in 722 BC. See 2 Kings 17–18.

e 7:37 When man's feasting is over there is still thirst. Jesus comes at the last day of the feast to satisfy the thirst of those who seek God. Only the Lord Jesus can quench the spiritual thirst of men by giving them his living water.

f 7:38 The root word used here is the same as the River Jordan, which means "flowing (down)."

g 7:38 Or "rivers of living water will flow from his throne within." See Isaiah 44:3, 55:1, 58:11, Ezekiel 47:1, and Revelation 22:1. A drink becomes a river!

h 7:39 As translated from the Aramaic.

out upon them, because Jesus had not yet been unveiled in his full splendor.[a]

Divided Opinions About Jesus

[40]When the crowd heard Jesus' words, some said, "This man really is a prophet!" [41]Others said, "He's the Messiah!" But others said, "How could he be the Anointed One since he's from Galilee? [42]Don't the Scriptures say that he will be one of David's descendants and be born in Bethlehem, the city of David?"[b] [43]So the crowd was divided over Jesus, [44]some wanted him arrested but no one dared to lay a hand on him.

The Unbelief of Religious Leaders

[45]So when the temple guards returned to the Pharisees and the leading priests without Jesus, they were questioned, "Where is he? Why didn't you bring that man back with you?"

[46]They answered, "You don't understand—he speaks amazing things like no one else has ever spoken!"

[47]The religious leaders mocked, "Oh, so now you also have been led astray by him? [48]Do you see even one of us, your leaders, following him? [49]This ignorant rabble swarms around him because none of them know anything about the Law! They're all cursed!"

[50]Just then, Nicodemus, who had secretly spent time with Jesus, spoke up, for he was a respected voice among them. [51]He cautioned them, saying, "Does our law decide a man's guilt before we first hear him and allow him to defend himself?"

---

a 7:39 This splendor included the splendor of the cross, the splendor of his resurrection, and the glory of his ascension into heaven. Just as water poured out of the rock that was struck by Moses, so from the wounded side of Jesus living water poured out to heal, save, and bring life to everyone who believes. The Holy Spirit poured out of Christ and into the church at Pentecost.

b 7:42 They had an understanding of the Bible but still missed who Jesus was. Bible knowledge alone, without the Holy Spirit opening our hearts and bringing us to Christ, can leave us as a skeptic. They jumped to conclusions, not realizing that Jesus may have been raised in Nazareth in Galilee, but he was born in Bethlehem and was a true descendant of David. See Psalm 89:3–4, Micah 5:2, Matthew 1:1 and 2:1, and Luke 2:4.

⁵²They argued, "Oh, so now you're an advocate for this Galilean! Search the Scriptures, Nicodemus, and you'll see that there's no mention of a prophet coming out of Galilee!"ᵃ *So with that their debate ended,* ⁵³and they each went their own way.

Eight

An Adulteress Forgiven

¹Jesus walked up the Mount of Olivesᵇ near the city *where he spent the night.* ²Then at dawn Jesus appeared in the temple courts again, and soon all the people gathered around to listen to his words, so he sat down and taught them. ³Then in the middle of his teaching, the religious scholarsᶜ and the Pharisees broke through the crowd and brought a woman who had been caught in the act of committing adultery and made her stand *in the middle* of everyone.

⁴Then they said to Jesus, "Teacher, we caught this woman in the very act of adultery. ⁵Doesn't Moses' Law command us to stone to death a woman like this?ᵈ Tell us, what do you say we should do with her?" ⁶They were only testing Jesus because they hoped to trap him with his own words and accuse him *of breaking the laws of Moses.*

---

a 7:52 They apparently didn't know their own Jewish history, for the prophet Jonah, in 580 BC, came from Gathepher, a village only three miles from Nazareth. It is believed that Elijah, Nahum, and Hosea also came from Galilee. Jesus' Galilean ministry was prophesied in Isaiah 9:1-2.

b 8:1 Named for the many olive trees on its slopes, the Mount of Olives was a high slope just east of Jerusalem across the Kidron Valley.

c 8:3 Or "scribes." The scribes were not merely professional copyists, they were the scholarly experts who were to be consulted over the details of the written Law of Moses.

d 8:4 See Leviticus 20:10 and Deuteronomy 22:22-24, where it is clear that both the man and woman was to be stoned to death.

But Jesus didn't answer them. Instead he simply bent down and wrote in the dust with his finger. [7]Angry, they kept insisting[a] that he answer their question, so Jesus stood up and looked at them and said, **"Let's have the man who has never had a sinful desire[b] throw the first stone at her."** [8]And then he bent over again and wrote some more words in the dust.[c]

[9]Upon hearing that, her accusers slowly left the crowd one at a time, beginning with the oldest to the youngest,[d] with a convicted conscience. [10]Until finally, Jesus was left alone with the woman still standing there in front of him. So he stood back up and said to her, **"Dear woman, where are your accusers? Is there no one here to condemn you?"**

[11]Looking around, she replied, "I see no one, Lord."[e]

Jesus said, **"Then I certainly[f] don't condemn you either.[g] Go, and from now on, be free from a life of sin."[h]**

---

a 8:7 As translated from the Aramaic.

b 8:7 The Greek word *anamartetos* means more than simply sin, but is best translated, "a sinful desire."

c 8:8 See Jeremiah 17:13. Jesus wrote in the dust to fulfill Jeremiah's prophecy that those who forsake God (spiritual adultery) will be written in the dust. All of the accusers were guilty of having forsaken God, the fountain of living water, and yet were so anxious to stone this woman to death. The same finger that wrote the Ten Commandments in stone also wrote the names of each of the accusers, or perhaps he wrote Jeremiah 17:13 in the dirt in front of their eyes, pointing to their hypocrisy.

d 8:9 The Aramaic can be translated, "starting with the priests."

e 8:11 The Aramaic contains a powerful testimony from this woman. Apparently the woman had the revelation of who Jesus really was, for she addressed Jesus with the divine name in the Aramaic, *MarYah*, LORD YAHWEH! See also 1 Corinthians 12:3. The Greek texts use the word *kurios* for Lord, which can also mean, "sir," or "land-owner."

f 8:11 The Greek has the emphatic use of the personal pronoun.

g 8:11 The Aramaic is, "Neither do I put you down (or, oppress you)." The Torah required two witnesses. There were none left!

h 8:11 Or "no longer be sinning." It should be noted that this entire episode (referred to commonly as the "Pericope Adulterae") is missing in the majority of the most reliable Greek manuscripts. There are some manuscripts that have this story at the end of the book of John and at least two that include it in the gospel of Luke. Many scholars surmise that this episode in the ministry of Jesus was added after the gospel of John had been completed. However, it is the conclusion of this translation that the above text is indeed an inspired account of the ministry of Jesus and may have been deleted by many translators and copyists who doubted that Jesus could tell an adulterer that he would not condemn her. St. Augustine, one of the early church fathers, mentioned this story and stated that many translators had removed it because they interpreted it as Jesus giving license to immorality. God's grace always seems to startle the religious. (St. Augustine, De Conjug. Adult., II:6.)

Jesus, the Light of the World

¹²Then Jesus said, "**I am**ᵃ **light to the world and those who embrace me will experience life-giving light, and they will never**ᵇ **walk**ᶜ **in darkness.**"

¹³The Pharisees were immediately offended and said, "You're just boasting about yourself! Since we only have your word on this, it makes your testimony invalid!"

¹⁴Jesus responded, "**Just because I am the one making these claims doesn't mean they're invalid.** *For I absolutely know who I am*, **where I've come from, and where I'm going. But you Pharisees have no idea about what I'm saying.** ¹⁵**For you've set yourselves up as judges of others based on outward appearances, but I certainly never judge others in that way.** ¹⁶**For I discern the truth. And I am not alone in my judgments, for my Father and I have the same understanding in all things, and he has sent me to you.**

¹⁷"**Isn't it written in the Law of Moses that the testimony of two men is trustworthy?**ᵈ ¹⁸**Then what I say about who I am is true, for I am not alone in my testimony—my Father is the other witness, and we testify together of the truth.**"

¹⁹Then they asked, "Just who is this 'Father' of yours? Where is he?"

Jesus answered, "**You wouldn't ask that question if you knew who I am, or my Father. For if you knew me, you would recognize my Father too.**" ²⁰(Jesus taught all these things while standing *in the treasure room of the temple.*ᵉ And no one dared to arrest him, for it wasn't yet his time to surrender to men.)

---

a 8:12 Again we see Jesus using the words, "I Am," which is the name of God.

b 8:12 The Greek word is a double negative, emphatically saying, "never, no never!"

c 8:12 The Aramaic is, "they will never be driven (pushed) by the darkness."

d 8:17 See Deuteronomy 17:6.

e 8:20 Jesus unlocks that "treasure room" to us, his temple. When we receive him as our life-giving light, we see the treasures that have been given to us by grace.

"I Am Not From This World"

²¹One day Jesus said again, **"I am about to leave you. You will want to find me, but you will still die in your sins.**ᵃ **You won't be able to come where I am going."**

²²This so confused the Jewish leaders that they began to say, "Is he planning to commit suicide? What's he talking about—'You won't be able to come where I am going'?"

²³Jesus spoke up and said, **"You are all from the earth; I am from above. I am not from this world like you are.** ²⁴**That's why I've told you that you will all die in your sins if you fail to believe that I Am who I Am."**ᵇ

²⁵So they asked him plainly, "Who are you?"

"I Am the One I've always claimed to be." Jesus replied. ²⁶**"And I still have many more things to pronounce in judgment about you. For I will testify to the world of the truths that I have heard from my Father, and the Father who sent me is trustworthy."** ²⁷(Even after all of this, they still didn't realize that he was speaking about his heavenly Father.)

²⁸**"You will know me as 'I Am' after you have lifted me up from the earth**ᶜ **as the Son of Man. Then you will realize that I do nothing on my own initiative, but I only speak the truth that the Father has revealed to me.** ²⁹**I am his messenger and he is always with me, for I only do that which delights his heart."**ᵈ ³⁰These words caused many *respected Jews* to believe in him.

---

a 8:21 Jesus gives a stern warning of dying before you have turned away from sin and put your faith in the Savior.

b 8:24 Believing the truth that Jesus Christ is the "I Am," God who became a man, is an essential part of our faith as followers of Christ.

c 8:28 There is a dual meaning in these words. To honor Jesus and exalt him reveals his true identity to our hearts. The word for *lifted up* can also mean "to exalt" and therefore, "to honor." However, Jesus was *lifted up* on a cross, suspended between heaven and earth, and died for the sins of all mankind. Both of these implications are found in this saying of Jesus.

d 8:29 The Aramaic is, "I only do what adorns (beautifies) him."

The Son Gives Freedom

³¹Jesus said to those Jews who believed in him, **"When you continue to embrace all that I teach, you prove that you are my true followers. ³²For if you embrace the truth, it will release more freedom into your lives."**[a]

³³Surprised by this, they said, "But we're the descendants of Abraham and we're already free. We've never been in bondage[b] to anyone. How could you say that we will be released into more freedom?"[c]

³⁴**"I speak eternal truth,"** Jesus said. **"When you sin you are not free. You've become a slave in bondage to your sin. ³⁵And slaves have no permanent standing in a family, like a son does, for a son is a part of the family forever. ³⁶So if the Son sets you free from sin, then become a true son and be unquestionably free! ³⁷Even though you are descendants of Abraham, you desire to kill me because the message I bring has not found a home in your hearts. ³⁸Yet the truths I speak I've seen and received in my Father's presence. But you are doing what you've learned from your father!"**[d]

³⁹"What do mean?" they replied. "Abraham is our father!"

Jesus said, **"If you are really Abraham's sons, then you would follow in the steps of Abraham. ⁴⁰I've only told you the truth that I've heard in my Father's presence, but now you are wanting me dead—is that how Abraham acted? ⁴¹No, you people are doing what your father has taught you!"**

Indignant, they responded, "What are you talking about? We only have one Father, God himself! We're not illegitimate!"

---

a 8:32 The truth Jesus gives us releases us from the bondage of our past, the bondage of our sins, and the bondage of religion. Jesus is speaking these words to those who were not fully free from man's traditions. Truth must be embraced and worked out through the divine process of spiritual maturity. The Greek word for "truth" is *reality*. To embrace the reality of Christ brings more freedom into your life. See the book of Galatians for a clear explanation of the freedom Jesus refers to here.

b 8:33 The Greek is translated, "slavery." However, the Aramaic word used here (*abdota*) refers not to slavery but to paying off debts (indentured servants). The Jews were not forgetting their slavery in Egypt, but rather saying that they were not in bondage to serve anyone as free sons of Abraham. Jesus reminds them that ancestral lineage does not guarantee spiritual freedom.

c 8:33 The Aramaic is translated, "released as children of freedom."

d 8:38 Some Greek manuscripts have, "since I'm saying what I've seen while with my Father, put my Father's words into practice."

⁴²Jesus said, "Then if God were really your father, you would love me, for I've come from his presence. I didn't come here on my own, but God sent me to you. ⁴³Why don't you understand what I say?ᵃ You don't understand because your hearts are closed to my message!

⁴⁴"You are the offspring of your father, the devil,ᵇ and you serve your father very well, passionately carrying out his desires. He's been a murderer right from the start! He never stood with the One who is the True Prince, for he's full of nothing but lies—lying is his native tongue.ᶜ He is a master of deception and the father of lies! ⁴⁵But I am the True Prince who speaks nothing but the truth, yet you refuse to believe and you want nothing to do with me. ⁴⁶Can you name one sin that I've committed? Then if I am telling you only the truth, why don't you believe me? ⁴⁷If you really knew God, you would listen, receive, and respond with faith to his words. But since you don't listen and respond to what he says, it proves you don't belong to him and you have no room for him in your hearts."

⁴⁸"See! We were right all along!" some of the Jewish leaders shouted. "You're nothing but a demon-possessed Samaritan!"ᵈ

⁴⁹Jesus replied, "It is not a demon that would cause me to honor my Father. I live my life for his honor, even though you insult me for it.ᵉ ⁵⁰I never have a need to seek my own glory, for the Father will do that for me, and he will judge those who do not. ⁵¹I speak to you this eternal truth: whoever cherishes my words and keeps them will never experience death."

---

a 8:43 The Aramaic is, "Why don't you receive my manifestation?"

b 8:44 The word for *devil* in Greek means "slanderer-accuser." The Aramaic word is *akelqarsa*, or "adversary." It is taken from a root word that means "to ridicule," or "to gnaw." See verse 48 where the Jewish leaders ridiculed Jesus' words.

c 8:44 Or "when he lies he's only doing what is natural to him."

d 8:48 They are obviously scorning Jesus by calling him a demon-possessed Samaritan. The Jews despised their northern cousins, the Samaritans, for their ancestors had come from Assyria and occupied Israel's lands. The three major groups in Israel at that time were Judeans (Jews), Galileans, and Samaritans. The Jerusalem Jews saw themselves as superior and more faithful to the God of the Hebrews than their northern neighbors. Jesus was a Galilean, having come from Nazareth. But Nazareth was part of the northern region looked down upon by the Jews. The Aramaic can be translated, "You're a crazy Samaritan."

e 8:49 The Aramaic is, "you curse me."

⁵²This prompted the Jewish leaders to say, "Now we know for sure that you're demon possessed! You just said that those who keep watch over your words will never experience death, but Abraham and all the prophets have died! ⁵³Do you think you're greater than our father Abraham and all the prophets? You are so delusional about yourself that you make yourself greater than you are!"

⁵⁴Jesus answered them, **"If I were to tell you how great I am, it would mean nothing. But my Father is the One who will prove it and will glorify me. Isn't he the One you claim is your God? ⁵⁵But in reality, you've never embraced him as your own. I know him, and I would be a liar, like yourselves, if I told you anything less than that. I have fully embraced him, and I treasure his every word. ⁵⁶And not only that, Abraham, your ancestor, was overjoyed when he received the revelation of my coming to earth. Yes, he foresaw me coming and was filled with delight!"**[a]

⁵⁷But many of the Jewish leaders doubted him and said, "What are you talking about? You're not even fifty years old yet. You talk like you've seen Abraham!"

⁵⁸Jesus said to them, **"I give you this eternal truth: I have existed long before Abraham was born, for I Am!"**[b]

⁵⁹When they heard this, they picked up rocks to stone him, but Jesus concealed himself as he passed through the crowd[c] and went away from there.

---

a 8:56 This refers to the prophetic insight God gave to Abraham about the coming Messiah. Many Hebrew scholars believe this was given to Abraham on the day of "binding." That is, the day he tied his son, Isaac, to the altar to offer him as a sacrifice. It was then that God showed him a ram that was caught in a thicket nearby to be the substitute for Isaac. See Galatians 3:16 and Hebrews 11:13.

b 8:58 Proper English grammar would be, "Before Abraham was born, I Was." However, Jesus identifies himself with the "I Am that I Am" of Exodus 3, when Yahweh appeared to Moses in the flames of the sacred shrub.

c 8:59 Some reliable Greek texts present Jesus' exit in a less than supernatural way. But the Aramaic and many other Greek manuscripts make it clear that it was a supernatural exit from the Jewish leaders who wanted to kill him. See also Luke 4:30 for another incident of Jesus walking through a hostile crowd. Chapter 8 begins with the self-righteous wanting to stone the adulterous woman, and ends with them wanting to stone the sinless Messiah.

Nine

___

Jesus Healed a Man Born Blind

¹Afterward, as Jesus walked down the street, he noticed a man blind from birth. ²His disciples asked him, "Teacher, whose sin caused this guy's blindness, his own, or the sin of his parents?"

³Jesus answered, **"Neither. It happened to him so that you could watch him experience God's miracle. ⁴While I am with you, it is daytime and we must do the works of God who sent me while the light shines. For there is coming a dark night when no one will be able to work.**ᵃ ⁵**As long as I am with you my life is the light that pierces the world's darkness."**

⁶Then Jesus spat on the ground and made some clay with his saliva.ᵇ Then he anointed the blind man's eyes with the clay. ⁷And he said to the blind man, **"Now go and wash the clay from your eyes in the ritual pool of Siloam."**ᶜ So he went and washed his face and as he came back, he could see for the first time in his life!ᵈ

⁸This caused quite a stir among the people of the neighborhood, for they noticed the blind beggar was now seeing! They began to say to one

___

a 9:4 The Aramaic can be translated, "The One who sent me is the day, and we must do his works. But the night (of mankind) will follow when no work can be accomplished."

b 9:6 John has left us a book of pictures. The picture here is the mingling of spit and clay, a picture of the Christ who is God and man. The saliva comes from the mouth, the spoken Word, God incarnate. The clay is always a picture of man, for our human vessel is a jar of clay. No doubt, the blind man had heard people spit as they walked by him, as a sign of disgust, for in that day they believed blindness was caused by a curse. But this day, as he heard Jesus spit on the ground, it was for his healing.

c 9:7 Or "the Pool of Apostleship." *Siloam* is a Hebrew word that means, "to be sent," or "to be commissioned," the Greek word for apostle or apostleship is the closest meaning. The apostle of our faith is the Lord Jesus Christ who was sent from the Father. To wash in the Pool of Apostleship is to recognize the healing that flows from the One who was sent from heaven.

d 9:7 In the context of Jesus' teaching on the light of the world and mankind being in the dark, this miracle of giving sight to the blind man is a powerful proof of Jesus' words. Christ, in his birth, became a man of clay. When he applies this clay over our eyes and we wash in the water of his Word, our spiritual sight is restored.

another, "Isn't this the blind man who once sat and begged?" [9]Some said, "No, it can't be him!" Others said, "But it looks just like him—it has to be him!" All the while the man kept insisting, "I'm the man who was blind!"

[10]Finally, they asked him, "What has happened to you?"

[11]He replied, "I met the man named Jesus! He rubbed clay on my eyes and said, 'Go to the pool named Siloam and wash.' So I went and while I was washing the clay from my eyes I began to see *for the very first time ever!*"[a]

[12]So the people of the neighborhood inquired, "Where is this man?"

"I have no idea." the man replied.

[13]So the people marched him over to the Pharisees to speak with them. [14]They were concerned because the miracle Jesus performed by making clay with his saliva and anointing the man's eyes happened on a Sabbath day, a day that no one was allowed to "work."

[15]Then the Pharisees asked the man, "How did you have your sight restored?"

He replied, "A man anointed my eyes with clay, then I washed, and now I can see for the first time in my life!"

[16]Then an argument broke out among the Pharisees over the healing of the blind man on the Sabbath. Some said, "This man who performed this healing is clearly not from God! He doesn't even observe the Sabbath!" Others said, "If Jesus is just an ordinary sinner,[b] how could he perform a miracle like that?"

[17]This prompted them to turn on the man healed of blindness, putting him on the spot in front of them all, demanding an answer. They asked, "Who do you say he is—this man who opened your blind eyes?"

"He's a prophet of God!" the man replied.

[18]Still refusing to believe that the man had been healed and was truly blind from birth, the Jewish leaders called for the man's parents to be brought to them.

---

a 9:11 See also verse 7 and 16.

b 9:16 Or "a sinning man."

19-20So they asked his parents, "Is this your son?"

"Yes," they answered.

"Was he really born blind?"

"Yes, he was," they replied.

So they pressed his parents to answer, "Then how is it that he's now seeing?"

21"We have no idea," they answered. "We don't know what happened to our son. Ask him, he's a mature adult. He can speak for himself." 22(Now the parents were obviously intimidated by the Jewish religious leaders, for they had already announced to the people that if anyone publicly confessed Jesus as the Messiah, they would be excommunicated. 23That's why they told them, "Ask him, he's a mature adult. He can speak for himself.")

24So once again they summoned the man who was healed of blindness and said to him, "Swear to God to tell us the truth!ᵃ We know the man who healed you is a sinful man! Do you agree?"

25The healed man replied, "I have no idea what kind of man he is. All I know is that I was blind and now I can see for the first time in my life!"

26"But what did he do to you?" they asked. "How did he heal you?"

27The man responded, "I told you once and you didn't listen to me. Why do you make me repeat it? Are you wanting to be his followers too?"

28This angered the Jewish leaders. They heaped insults on him, "We can tell you are one of his followers—now we know it! We are true followers of Moses, 29for we know that God spoke to Moses directly. But as for this one, we don't know where he's coming from!"

30"Well, what a surprise this is!" the man said. "You don't even know where he comes from, but he healed my eyes and now I can see! 31We know that God doesn't listen to sinners, but only to godly people who do his will. 32Yet who has ever heard of a man born blind that was healed

---

a 9:24 Or "give glory to God." This has been interpreted by some as an idiomatic saying, which would put the man under oath to testify the truth.

and given back his eyesight? ³³I tell you, if this man isn't from God, he wouldn't be able to heal me like he has!"

³⁴Some of the Jewish leaders were enraged and said, "Just who do you think you are to lecture us! You were born a blind, filthy sinner!" So they threw the man out in the street.

³⁵When Jesus learned they had thrown him out, he went to find him and said to him, **"Do you believe in the Son of God?"**[a]

³⁶The man whose blind eyes were healed answered, "Who is he, Master? Tell me so that I can place all my faith in him."

³⁷Jesus replied, **"You're looking right at him. He's speaking with you. It's me, the one in front of you now."**

³⁸Then the man threw himself at his feet and worshipped Jesus and said, "Lord, I believe in you!"[b]

³⁹And Jesus said, **"I have come to judge those who think they see and make them blind. And for those who are blind, I have come to make them see."**

⁴⁰Some of the Pharisees were standing nearby and overheard these words. They interrupted Jesus and said, "You mean to tell us that we are blind?"

⁴¹Jesus told them, **"If you would acknowledge your blindness, then your sin would be removed. But now that you claim to see, your sin remains with you!"**[c]

---

a 9:35 This is a common title of the Lord Jesus in the book of John. Although there are many reliable Greek manuscripts that have "the Son of Man," the Aramaic and a few early Greek manuscripts have "the Son of Elohim (God)."

b 9:38 Although this man had never been able to read the Scriptures, he had faith in Jesus. Traditions and superficial knowledge of the Bible can actually blind our hearts if we do not believe in Jesus above all other religious dogmas. Many of those who knew the Scriptures refused to believe. The miracle of blind eyes opening is proof that God had come to us. See Isaiah 35:4-5.

c 9:41 Or "your sin stands (rises up)."

Ten

The Parable of the Kind Shepherd

¹Jesus said to the Pharisees, **"Listen to this eternal truth: The person who sneaks over the wall to enter into the sheep pen, rather than coming through the gate, reveals himself as a thief coming to steal.** ²**But the True Shepherd walks right up to the gate,** ³**and because the gatekeeper knows who he is, he opens the gate to let him in.**ᵃ **And the sheep recognize the voice of the True Shepherd, for he calls his own by name and leads them out, for they belong to him.** ⁴**And when he has brought out all his sheep, he walks ahead of them and they will follow him, for they are familiar with his voice.** ⁵**But they will run away from strangers and never follow them because they know it's the voice of a stranger."** ⁶Jesus told the Pharisees this parable even though they didn't understand a word of what he meant.ᵇ

⁷So Jesus went over it again, **"I speak to you eternal truth: I am the Gate for the flock.**ᶜ ⁸**All those who broke in before me are thieves who came to steal,**ᵈ **but the sheep never listened to them.** ⁹**I am the Gateway.**ᵉ

---

a 10:3 In this parable the gatekeeper would represent John the Immerser who recognized Jesus as the shepherd. John opened the gate for him to be introduced to Israel at Jesus' baptism.

b 10:6 They didn't understand this allegory of the Old Testament Law as the sheepfold that became the religion of Judaism, like a pen that confined the people. Christ is the gate that not only allowed everyone in, but he let them out in the New Testament to enjoy all the riches of the pasture. The Holy Spirit is the gatekeeper and the false prophets and Pharisees are the thieves and robbers. Remember that this chapter follows the healing of the blind man who was cast out of the "sheep pen" but accepted in Christ. See Galatians 3:23–26. Jesus is the shepherd, the gate, and the pasture.

c 10:7 As translated from the Aramaic. There is a word play with "I" (ena) and "flock" (ana). As the gateway, he brings us to the Father and his kingdom realm. As the shepherd, he cares for us and shows us his loving heart.

d 10:8 The Old Testament refers to the kings of Israel and Judah as "shepherds." These kings along with false prophets are shepherds who don't always have God's heart for the sheep. After the healing of the blind man, the Pharisees refused to acknowledge Jesus' rightful place as shepherd of his flock, so the *thieves coming to steal* would also refer to them.

e 10:9 A sheep pen was an enclosure with walls and no roof that would often have the sheep of an entire village kept within. After the sheep were brought in for the night, it was common for the shepherd to sleep at the entrance so he could protect his sheep. Only the shepherds of the sheep would

To enter through me is to experience life, freedom, and satisfaction.[a] [10]A thief has only one thing in mind—he wants to steal, slaughter,[b] and destroy. But I came to *give you everything in abundance,*[c] *more than you expect*[d]—life in its fullness until you overflow! [11]"I am the Good[e] Shepherd who lays down my life as a sacrifice for the sheep. [12-13]But the worker who serves only for wages is not a real shepherd. Because he has no heart for the sheep he will run away and abandon them when he sees the wolf coming. And then the wolf mauls the sheep, drags them off, and scatters them.

[14]"I alone am the Good Shepherd, and I know those whose hearts are mine, for they recognize me and know me, [15]just as my Father knows my heart and I know my Father's heart. I am ready to give my life for the sheep.

[16]"And I have other sheep that I will gather which are not of this Jewish flock. And I, their shepherd, must lead them too, and they will follow me and listen to my voice. And I will join them all into one flock with one shepherd.[f]

[17]"The Father has an intense love for me because I freely give my own life—to raise it up again. [18]I surrender my own life, and no one has the power to take my life from me. I have the authority to lay it down and the power to take it back again. This is the destiny my Father has set before me."

[19]This teaching set off another heated controversy among the Jewish

---

be recognized by that gatekeeper. Jesus is the one who will remain with his flock and keep his sheep living in peace and safety. His teaching (voice) will guard us from the unreliable teachers who want to steal our hearts and bind us to themselves. They steal and rob the affection that belongs only to Jesus, our kind shepherd.

a 10:9 Or "go in and out and find pasture."

b 10:10 The Greek word *thuo* is not the usual word for "kill." It means "sacrifice," or "slaughter."

c 10:10 Implied in the Aramaic text.

d 10:10 Implied in the Greek text.

e 10:11 The word for "good" in Greek (*kalos*) can also mean beautiful, virtuous, excellent, genuine, or better. See Strong's Concordance #2570. Jesus is also called the "Great Shepherd" (Hebrews 13:20) and the "Chief Shepherd" (1 Peter 5:4).

f 10:16 This "one flock" is the church made up of both Jew and non-Jew. See Ephesians 2:11-14 and Ezekiel 34:23.

leaders. [20]Many of them said, "This man is a demon-possessed lunatic! Why would anyone listen to a word he says?" [21]But then there were others who weren't so sure: "His teaching is full of insight. These are not the ravings of a madman! How could a demonized man give sight to one born blind?"

Jesus at the Feast of Renewal

[22-23]The time came to observe the winter Feast of Renewal in Jerusalem.[a] Jesus walked into the temple area under Solomon's covered walkway [24]when the Jewish leaders encircled him and said, "How much longer will you keep us in suspense? Tell us the truth and clarify this for us once and for all. Are you really the Messiah, the Anointed One?"

[25]Jesus answered them, **"I have told you the truth already and you did not believe me. The proof of who I am is revealed by all the miracles that I do in the name of my Father. [26]Yet, you stubbornly refuse to follow me, because you are not my sheep. As I've told you before: [27]'My own sheep will hear my voice and I know each one, and they will follow me.' [28]I give to them the gift of eternal life and they will never be lost and no one has the power to snatch them out of my hands. [29]My Father, who has given them to me as his gift, is the mightiest of all, and no one has the power to snatch them from my Father's care. [30]The Father and I are one."**

[31]When they heard this, the Jewish leaders were so enraged that they picked up rocks to stone him to death. [32]But Jesus said, **"My Father has empowered me to work many miracles and acts of mercy among you. So which one of them do you want to stone me for?"**

[33]The Jewish leaders responded, "We're not stoning you for any-thing good you did—it's because of your blasphemy! You're just *a son of Adam*, but you've claimed to be God!"

[34]Jesus answered, **"Isn't it written in your Scriptures that God said,**

---

a 10:22–23 This is also known as the "Feast of Dedication," or "The Feast of Lights." Contemporary Judaism recognizes this as Hanukkah. The Greek is literally "The Feast of Renewing," to commemo-rate the miraculous renewing of oil that burned for eight days.

'You are gods?'[a] The Scriptures cannot be denied or found to be in error. [35]So if those who have the message of the Scriptures are said to be 'gods,' then why would you accuse me of blasphemy? [36]For I have been uniquely chosen by God and he is the one who sent me to you. How then could it be blasphemy for me to say, 'I am the Son of God!' [37]If I'm not doing the beautiful works that my Father sent me to do, then don't believe me. [38]But if you see me doing the beautiful works of God upon the earth, then you should at least believe the evidence of the miracles, even if you don't believe my words! Then you would come to experience me and be convinced that I am in the Father and the Father is in me."

[39]Once again they attempted to seize him, but he escaped *miraculously*[b] from their clutches. [40]Then Jesus went back to the place where John had baptized him at the crossing of the Jordan. [41]Many came out to where he was and said about him, "Even though John didn't perform any miracles, everything he predicted about this man is true!" [42]And many people became followers of Jesus at the Jordan and believed in him.

Eleven

Lazarus Raised from the Dead

[1-2]In the village of Bethany there was a man named Lazarus, and his sisters, Miriam and Martha. Miriam was the one who would anoint Jesus' feet with costly perfume and dry his feet with her long hair. One day Lazarus

---

a 10:34 See Psalm 82:6.

b 10:39 Implied in the context of being encircled by those with stones in their hands ready to kill him. It was clearly a miracle. He may have become invisible, transported himself to another location, or caused his accusers to be momentarily paralyzed or blinded as he slipped away.

became very sick to the point of death. ³So his sisters sent *a message* to Jesus, "Lord, our brother Lazarus, the one you love, is very sick. Please come!"

⁴When he heard this, he said, **"This sickness will not end in death for Lazarus, but will bring glory and praise to God. This will reveal the greatness of the Son of God by what takes place."**

⁵⁻⁶Now even though Jesus loved Miriam, Martha, and Lazarus, he remained where he was for two more days. ⁷Finally, on the third day, he said to his disciples, **"Come. It's time to go to Bethany."**ᵃ

⁸"But Teacher," they said to him, "do you really want to go back there? It was just a short time ago the people of Judea were going to stone you!"

⁹⁻¹⁰Jesus replied, **"Are there not twelve hours of daylight *in every day*?ᵇ You can go through a day without the fear of stumbling when you walk in the One who gives light to the world. But you will stumble when the light is not in you, for you'll be walking in the dark.**

¹¹Then Jesus added, **"Lazarus, our friend, has just fallen asleep.ᶜ It's time that I go and awaken him."**

¹²When they heard this, the disciples replied, "Lord, if he has just fallen asleep, then he'll get better." ¹³Jesus was speaking about Lazarus' death, but the disciples presumed he was talking about natural sleep.

¹⁴Then Jesus made it plain to them, **"Lazarus is dead. ¹⁵And for your sake, I'm glad I wasn't there, *because now you have another opportunity to see who I am* so that you will learn to trust in me. Come, let's go and see him."**

¹⁶So Thomas, nicknamed the Twin, remarked to the other disciples, "Let's go so that we can die with him."ᵈ

---

a 11:7 Or "Judea."

b 11:9-10 Jesus uses a parable to respond to why he is not afraid to go where his life could be in danger. This is more than the sun, but "the One who gives light to the world."

c 11:11 Jesus is stating an obvious euphemism. Lazarus "sleeping" means that he has died. To "awaken" him means that Jesus would raise him from the dead.

d 11:16 It is likely that Thomas was expressing pessimism about the fate of Jesus going back into the region where he was threatened with death.

17-18Now when they arrived at Bethany, which was only about two miles from Jerusalem, Jesus found that Lazarus had already been in the tomb for four days. 19Many friends[a] of Miriam and Martha had come from the region to console them over the loss of their brother. 20And when Martha heard that Jesus was approaching the village, she went out to meet him, but Miriam stayed in the house.

21Martha said to Jesus, "My Lord, if only you had come sooner, my brother wouldn't have died. 22But I know that if you were to ask God for anything, he would do it for you."

23Jesus told her, **"Your brother will rise and live."**

24She replied, "Yes, I know he will rise with everyone else on resurrection day."[b]

25**"Martha,"** Jesus said, *"You don't have to wait until then.* **I am[c] the Resurrection,[d] and I am Life Eternal. Anyone who clings to me in faith, even though he dies, will live forever. 26And the one who lives by believing in me will never die.[e] Do you believe this?"** [f]

27Then Martha replied, "Yes, Lord, I do! I've always believed that you are the Anointed One, the Son of God who has come into the world for us!" 28Then she left and hurried off to her sister, Miriam, and called her aside from all the mourners and whispered to her, "He's here! And he wants to speak with you."

29So when Miriam heard this, she quickly went off to find him, 30for Jesus was lingering outside the village at the same spot where Martha met

---

a 11:19 Or "Jews."

b 11:24 Or "at the last day."

c 11:25 The words *I am* in the Aramaic are a clear statement of Christ's deity, "I am the Living God, the Resurrection and the Life!"

d 11:25 The Aramaic uses a word that is related linguistically to the name *Noah*, who was symbolically "resurrected" from the flood as the life-giver to those who re-populated the earth. Resurrection is superior to life, for life can be defeated and ended. But resurrection overcomes. Life is the power to exist, but resurrection is the power to conquer all, even death itself. Believers must learn to live in Christ our Life, but also, Christ our Resurrection to conquer all things. See Philippians 3:10.

e 11:26 This is very emphatic in the Greek, "never die forever!"

f 11:26 John presents Jesus as the great Savior who saves us from sin (John 8), blindness (John 9–10), and death (John 11).

him. ³¹Now when Miriam's friends who were comforting her[a] noticed how quickly she ran out of the house, they followed her, assuming she was going to the tomb of her brother to mourn.

³²When Miriam finally found Jesus outside the village, she fell at his feet in tears and said, "Lord, if only you had been here, my brother would not have died."

³³When Jesus looked at Miriam and saw her weeping at his feet, and all her friends who were with her grieving, he shuddered with emotion[b] and was deeply moved with tenderness and compassion. ³⁴He said to them, **"Where did you bury him?"**

"Lord, come with us and we'll show you," they replied.

³⁵Then tears streamed down Jesus' face.

³⁶Seeing Jesus weep caused many of the mourners to say, "Look how much he loved Lazarus."[c] ³⁷Yet others said, "Isn't this the One who opens blind eyes? Why didn't he do something to keep Lazarus from dying?"

³⁸Then Jesus, with intense emotions, came to the tomb—a cave with a stone placed over its entrance. ³⁹Jesus told them, **"Roll away the stone."**

Then Martha said, "But Lord, it's been four days since he died—by now his body is already decomposing!"

⁴⁰Jesus looked at her and said, **"Didn't I tell you that if you will believe in me, you will see God unveil his power?"**[d]

⁴¹So they rolled away the heavy stone. Jesus gazed into heaven and said, **"Father, thank you that you have heard my prayer, ⁴²for you listen to every word I speak. Now, so that these who stand here with me will believe that you have sent me to the earth as your messenger, *I will use the power you have given me.*"** ⁴³Then with a loud voice Jesus shouted with authority: **"Lazarus! Come out of the tomb!"**

---

a 11:31 The Aramaic is, "Miriam (Mary)'s friends who loved her."

b 11:33 The Greek word used here (*enebrimēsato*) can also mean, "indignant and stirred with anger." Was he angry at the mourners? Not at all. He was angry over the work of the devil in taking the life of his friend, Lazarus. The Aramaic, however, has no connotation of indignation, only tenderness and compassion (literally, "his heart melted with compassion").

c 11:36 The Aramaic is, "how much mercy he felt for Lazarus."

d Or "you would see the glory of God."

⁴⁴Then in front of everyone, Lazarus, who had died four days earlier, slowly hobbled out—he still had grave clothes tightly wrapped around his hands and feet and covering his face! Jesus said to them, **"Unwrap him and let him loose."**ᵃ

⁴⁵From that day forward many of thoseᵇ who had come to visit Miriam believed in him, for they had seen with their own eyes this amazing miracle! ⁴⁶But a few went back to inform the Pharisees about what Jesus had done.

⁴⁷So the Pharisees and the chief priests called a special meeting of the High Councilᶜ and said, "So what are we going to do about this man? Look at all the great miracles he's performing! ⁴⁸If we allow him to continue like this, everyone will believe in him. And the Romans will take action and destroy both our country and our people!"ᵈ

⁴⁹Now Caiaphas, the high priest that year, spoke up and said, "You don't understand a thing! ⁵⁰Don't you realize we'd be much better off if this one man were to die for the people than for the whole nation to perish?"

⁵¹(This prophecy that Jesus was destined to dieᵉ for the Jewish people didn't come from Caiaphas himself, *but he was moved by God* to prophesy as the chief priest. ⁵²And Jesus' death would not be for the Jewish people only, but to gather together God's children scattered around the world and unite them as one.)ᶠ ⁵³So from that day on, they were committed to killing Jesus.

⁵⁴For this reason Jesus no longer went out in public among the Jews.

---

a 11:44 Burial customs in the Middle East were to wrap the corpse in white cotton cloths from the neck to the feet. The head was then covered with a large handkerchief.

b 11:45 Or "Jews."

c 11:47 Or "the Sanhedrin." This was the Great Sanhedrin, equivalent to a Jewish court, which would be comprised of seventy men who would judge Jewish religious matters.

d 11:48 As translated from the Aramaic. The Greek is translated, "our place (position) and our nation." "Our place" could refer to the temple.

e 11:51 As translated from the Aramaic.

f 11:52 See Isaiah 49:6.

But he went in the wilderness to a village called Ephraim,[a] where he secluded himself with his disciples.

⁵⁵Now the time came for the Passover preparations, and many from the countryside went to Jerusalem for their ceremonial cleansing before the feast began. ⁵⁶And all the people kept looking out for Jesus, expecting him to come to the city. They said to themselves while they waited in the temple courts, "Do you think that he will dare come to the feast?" ⁵⁷For the leading priests and the Pharisees had given orders that they be informed immediately if anyone saw Jesus, so they could seize and arrest him.

Twelve

Miriam Anoints Jesus

¹Six days before the Passover began, Jesus went back to Bethany, the town where he raised Lazarus from the dead. ²They had prepared a supper for Jesus.[b] Martha served, and Lazarus and Miriam were among those at the table. ³Miriam picked up an alabaster[c] jar filled with nearly a liter[d] of extremely rare and costly perfume—the purest extract of nard,[e] and she anointed Jesus' feet. Then she wiped them dry with her long hair. And

---

a 11:54 The Aramaic can be translated, "the fortress city of Ephraim," or "the mill called Ephraim." Ephraim means "double fruitfulness." Some believe this location is the present town of Et-Taiyibeh, which would make it about 14 miles (22 km) northeast of Jerusalem.

b 12:2 We see from Mark 14:3 that this took place at the house of Simon, the leper Jesus had healed.

c 12:3 As translated from the Aramaic.

d 12:3 Or "nearly a pound."

e 12:3 Nard is an extremely expensive perfume taken from the root and spike of the nard plant found in northern India. See Song of Songs 1:12, 4:13–14.

the fragrance of the costly oil filled the house.[a] [4]But Judas the locksmith,[b] Simon's son, the betrayer, spoke up and said, [5]"What a waste! We could have sold this perfume for a fortune[c] and given the money to the poor!"

[6](In fact, Judas had no heart for the poor. He only said this because he was a thief and in charge of the money case. He would steal money whenever he wanted from the funds *given to support Jesus' ministry*.)

[7]Jesus said to Judas, **"Leave her alone! She has saved it for the time of my burial.[d] [8]You'll always have the poor with you;[e] but you won't always have me."**

[9]When the word got out that Jesus was not far from Jerusalem, a large crowd came out to see him, and they also wanted to see Lazarus, the man Jesus had raised from the dead. [10]This prompted the chief priests to seal their plans to do away with both Jesus and Lazarus,[f] [11]for his miracle testimony was incontrovertible and was persuading many of the Jews living in Jerusalem to believe in Jesus.

[12]The next day the news that Jesus was on his way to Jerusalem swept through the massive crowd gathered for the feast. [13]So they took palm branches[g] and went out to meet him. Everyone was shouting, "Lord, be our Savior![h] Blessed is the one who comes to us sent from Jehovah-God,[i] the King of Israel!"

---

a 12:3 This fragrance, usually associated with a king, was upon Jesus' feet as he stood before his accusers and as the soldiers pierced his feet with a nail. It is possible they would all have smelled the fragrance of this costly perfume.

b 12:4 Or "Iscariot," a word related linguistically to "a lock" or "locksmith." Judas apparently held the key to the lockbox of funds to support Jesus' ministry. See also 6:71.

c 12:5 Or "Three hundred silver coins (denarii)," which would be equal to a year's salary.

d 12:7 The Aramaic could be translated, "Let her conduct my burial day ceremony." It is possible that this rare and expensive perfume could have been her family's treasure or her inheritance.

e 12:8 That is, "You will have many opportunities to help the poor, but you will not always have me." See also Deuteronomy 15:11.

f 12:10 Darkness has only one way to deal with the truth—kill it.

g 12:13 The palm tree is a symbol of triumph, victory over death. Palms grow in the desert and overcome the arid climate. Deborah sat under a palm tree as a judge in Israel and received the strategy to overcome her enemies. See also Revelation 7:9.

h 12:13 Or "Hosanna!"

i 12:13 See Psalm 118:25–26.

¹⁴Then Jesus found a young donkey and rode on it to fulfill what was prophesied: ¹⁵**"People of Zion,**ᵃ **have no fear! Look—it's your king coming to you riding on a young donkey!"**ᵇ

¹⁶Now Jesus' disciples didn't fully understand the importance of what was taking place, but after he was raised and exalted into glory, they understood how Jesus fulfilled all the prophecies in the Scriptures that were written about him.

¹⁷All the eyewitnesses of the miracle Jesus performed when he called Lazarus out of the tomb and raised him from the dead kept spreading the news about Jesus to everyone. ¹⁸The news of this miracle of resurrection caused the crowds to swell as great numbers of people *welcomed him into the city with joy.*ᶜ ¹⁹But the Pharisees were disturbed by this and said to each other, "We won't be able to stop this.ᵈ The whole world is going to run after him!"

True Seekers

²⁰Now there were a number of foreigners from among the nations who were worshippers at the feast.ᵉ ²¹They went to Philip (who came from the village of Bethsaida in Galilee) and they asked him, "Would you take us to see Jesus? We want to see him." ²²So Philip went to find Andrew, and then they both went to inform Jesus.

²³He replied to them, **"Now is the time for the Son of Man to be glorified. ²⁴Let me make this clear:**ᶠ **A single grain of wheat will never be more than a single grain of wheat unless it drops into the ground and**

---

a 12:15 Or "daughter of Zion."

b 12:15 See Zechariah 9:9. Conquering kings would ride on a warhorse or in a golden chariot, but Jesus rode into Jerusalem on a domesticated donkey. He is the King of Peace.

c 12:18 The Greek is, "the crowd went out to meet him." The Aramaic is, "great crowds went in front of him."

d 12:19 The Aramaic is, "See, you have lost your influence."

e 12:20 As translated from the Aramaic. The Greek text states they were "Greeks."

f 12:24 The Aramaic is translated, "Timeless truth I say to you."

JOHN TWELVE • 69

dies. Because then it sprouts and produces[a] a great harvest of wheat—all because one grain[b] died.[c]

25"The person who loves his life and pampers himself will miss true life! But the one who detaches his life from this world and abandons himself to me, will find true life and enjoy it forever! 26If you want to be my disciple, follow me and you will go where I am going.[d] And if you truly follow me as my disciple,[e] the Father will shower his favor upon your life.

27"Even though I am torn within, and my soul is in turmoil, I will not ask the Father to rescue me from this hour of trial. For I have come to fulfill my purpose[f]—to offer myself to God. 28So, Father, bring glory to your name!"[g] Then suddenly a booming voice was heard from the sky,

"I have glorified my name! And I will glorify it through you again!"

29The audible voice of God startled the crowd standing nearby. Some thought it was only thunder, yet others said, "An angel just spoke to him!"

30Then Jesus told them, "The voice you heard was not for my benefit, but for yours—to help you believe. 31From this moment on, everything

---

a 12:24 The Aramaic has an interesting word play with "it dies" (*myta*) and "it produces" (*mytya*).

b 12:24 The "one grain" is Jesus Christ, who will within days be offered as the sacrifice for sin on Calvary's cross. He will "drop" into the ground as "a grain of wheat" and bring forth a great "harvest" of "seeds." This parable given to Philip and Andrew was meant to be Jesus' reply to the request by the non-Jewish seekers to see Jesus. Christ's answer? "They will see me through you. As you follow me, you will also experience the dying and birthing experience." The harvest among the nations will come when we follow Jesus where he goes.

c 12:24 The Aramaic is translated, "if it dies, it will bring forth a great rebirth."

d 12:26 The implication in the text is that a life of full surrender to God will make us "a grain of wheat" that multiplies into a "harvest." The Greek text can be translated, "If anyone ministers to me (materially provides for me), where I am, my minister will be there too."

e 12:26 Or "materially provides for me."

f The Aramaic is translated, "to fulfill this hour I have come."

g Some later manuscripts have, "Father, bring glory to your Son." One of the oldest manuscripts reads "Father, bring glory to your name with the glory that I had with you before the world was created." The majority of reliable manuscripts have, "Father, bring glory to your name."

in this world is about to change,[a] for the ruler[b] of this dark world will be overthrown.[c] 32*And I will do this* when I am lifted up off the ground[d] and when I draw the hearts of people[e] to gather them to me." 33He said this to indicate that he would die by being lifted up on the cross.[f]

34People from the crowd spoke up and said, "Die? How could the Anointed One die? The Word of God says that the Anointed One will live with us forever,[g] but you just said that the Son of Man must be lifted up from the earth.[h] And who is this Son of Man anyway?"

35Jesus replied, "You will have the light shining with you for only a little while longer. While you still have me, walk in the light, so that the darkness doesn't overtake you. For when you walk in the dark you have no idea where you're going. 36So believe and cling to the light while I am with you, so that you will become children of light." After saying this, Jesus then entered into the crowd and hid himself from them.

The Unbelief of the Crowd

37Even with the overwhelming evidence of all the many signs and wonders that Jesus had performed in front of them, his critics still refused to believe. 38This fulfilled the prophecy given by Isaiah:

> *Lord, who has believed our message? Who has seen the unveiling of your great power?*[i]

---

a 12:31 Or "the time of judging the world (system) has come." The judging of the world is the overthrow of the kingdom of darkness. The preaching of the gospel of Jesus Christ is passing a sentence of judgment on this fallen world and declaring treason in the kingdom of darkness. Everything changes because of the cross—the hinge of history.

b 12:31 An obvious reference to Satan.

c 12:31 Or "driven into exile."

d 12:32 The Aramaic phrase "lifted up" is another way of saying, "lifted up in crucifixion." The Greek implies being lifted up from beneath the earth (resurrection).

e 12:32 Or "I will draw all things to myself." Or "I will bundle everyone/everything next to me." Jesus also drew all our judgment to himself when he died for our sins. The Judge became the payment for the guilty.

f 12:33 Or "to clarify what kind of death he would die."

g 12:34 See Psalm 89:35–37, Isaiah 9:7, Ezekiel 37:25, and Daniel 7:14.

h 12:34 It was obvious to the crowd that Jesus being lifted up was a reference to the cross.

i 12:38 Or "To whom is the arm of the Lord revealed." The arm of the Lord is a metaphor for God's great power. The word for *revealed* means "to unveil." See Isaiah 53:1.

[39] And the people were not able to believe, for Isaiah also prophesied:

[40] *God has blinded their eyes and hardened their hearts*[a] *to the truth. So with their eyes and hearts closed they cannot understand the truth nor turn to me so that I could instantly cleanse and heal them.*[b]

[41] Isaiah said these things because he had seen and experienced the splendor of Jesus[c] and prophesied about him. [42] Yet there were many Jewish leaders who believed in Jesus, but because they feared the Pharisees they kept it secret, so they wouldn't be ostracized by the assembly of the Jews. [43] For they loved the glory that men could give them rather than the glory that came from God!

Jesus' Last Public Teaching

[44] Jesus shouted out passionately, **"To believe in me is to also believe in God who sent me. [45] For when you look at me you are seeing the One who sent me. [46] I have come as a light to shine in this dark world so that all who trust in me will no longer wander in darkness. [47] If you hear my words and refuse to follow them, I do not judge you. For I have not come to judge you but to save you. [48] If you reject me and refuse to follow my words,**[d] **you already have a judge. The message of truth I have given you will rise up to judge you at the Day of Judgment.**[e] **[49] For I'm not speaking as someone who is self-appointed, but I speak by the authority of the Father himself who sent me, and who instructed me what to say. [50] And I know that the Father's commandments result**[f] **in eternal life, and that's why I speak the very words I've heard him speak."**

---

a 12:40 Or "closed their minds." The Aramaic is translated, "darkened their hearts." The Aramaic indicates that they did this to themselves, rather than God doing this.

b 12:40 The Aramaic is translated "cleansed," the Greek is translated "healed." Both are included here. See Isaiah 6:10.

c 12:41 See Isaiah 6:1–5. This is a profound statement that Isaiah saw Jesus Christ when he was taken into heaven and encountered the Lord Yahweh on the throne. This "Lord high and exalted" was none less than Jesus Christ before he became a man.

d 12:48 This is the plural form of the Greek word *rhema*, and would refer to all that Jesus taught.

e 12:48 Or "at the last day."

f 12:50 Or in the Aramaic, "represent."

Thirteen

Jesus Washes Feet

¹Jesus knew that the night before Passover would be his last night on earth before leaving this world to return to the Father's side. All throughout his time with his disciples, Jesus had demonstrated a deep and tender love for them. And now he longed to show them the full measure of his love.[a] ²Before their evening meal had begun, the accuser[b] had already planted betrayal[c] into the heart of Judas Iscariot, the son of Simon.

³Now Jesus was fully aware that the Father had placed all things under his control, for he had come from God and was about to go back to be with him. ⁴So he got up from the meal and took off his outer robe, and took a towel and wrapped it around his waist. ⁵Then he poured water into a basin and began to wash the disciples' dirty feet and dry them with his towel.

⁶But when Jesus got to Simon Peter, he objected and said, "I can't let you wash my dirty feet—you're my Lord!"

⁷Jesus replied, **"You don't understand yet the meaning of what I'm doing, but soon it will be clear to you."**

⁸Peter looked at Jesus and said, "You'll never wash my dirty feet—never!"

"But Peter, if you don't allow me to wash your feet," Jesus responded, **"then you will not be able to share life with me."**

⁹So Peter the Rock said, "Lord, in that case, don't just wash my feet, wash my hands and my head too!"

¹⁰Jesus said to him, **"You are already clean. You've been washed**

---

a 13:1 Or "he loved them to the very end."

b 13:2 Or "devil."

c 13:2 Or "that he should betray Jesus." The Aramaic is, "Satan arose in the heart of Judas to betray Jesus."

completely and you just need your feet to be cleansed—but that can't be said of all of you." For Jesus knew which one was about to betray him, ¹¹and that's why he told them that not all of them were clean.

¹²After washing their feet, he put his robe on and returned to his place at the table.ª "Do you understand what I just did?" Jesus said. ¹³"You've called me your teacher and lord, and you're right, for that's who I am. ¹⁴⁻¹⁵So if I'm your teacher and lord and have just washed your dirty feet, then you should follow the example that I've set for you and wash one another's dirty feet. Now do for each other what I have just done for you. ¹⁶I speak to you timeless truth: a servant is not superior to his master, and an apostle is never greater than the one who sent him. ¹⁷So now put into practice what I have done for you, and you will experience a life of happiness enriched with untold blessings!"

Jesus Predicts His Betrayal

¹⁸"I don't refer to all of you when I tell you these things, for I know the ones I've chosen—to fulfill the Scripture that says, 'The one who shared supper with me treacherously betrays me.'ᵇ ¹⁹I am telling you this now, before it happens, so that when the prophecy comes to pass you will be convinced that I Am.ᶜ ²⁰"Listen to this timeless truth: whoever receives the messenger I send receives me, and the one who receives me receives the Fatherᵈ who sent me."

---

a 13:12 There has never been a nobleman, a teacher, or a king that loves and serves his servants like Jesus.

b 13:18 Or "has lifted up his heel against me." The Greek text preserves the idiom of Psalm 41:9, which speaks of a treacherous betrayal. In the Semitic culture, it is the greatest breach of etiquette to sit and eat with a friend and then later betray them. This is why many would never eat with someone they were not on good terms with. See also footnote on Psalm 41:9.

c 13:19 Or "I Am the one," or, "I Am Who I Am." Jesus once again equates himself with Jehovah God, the I Am.

d 13:20 Or "the One." By implication, this is the Father.

²¹Then Jesus was moved deeply in his spirit.ᵃ Looking at his disciples, he announced, **"I tell you the truth—one of you is about to betray me."**

²²Eyeing each other, his disciples puzzled over which one of them could do such a thing. ²³The disciple that Jesus dearly lovedᵇ was at the right of him at the tableᶜ and was leaning his head on Jesus. ²⁴Peter the Rock gestured to this disciple to ask Jesus who it was he was referring to. ²⁵Then the dearly loved disciple leaned into Jesus' chest and whispered, "Master, who is it?"

²⁶**"The one I give this piece of bread to after I've dipped it in the bowl,"** Jesus replied. Then he dipped the piece of bread into the bowl and handed it to Judas Iscariot, the son of Simon.ᵈ ²⁷And when Judas ate the piece of bread, Satanᵉ entered him. Then Jesus looked at Judas and said, **"What you are planning to do, go do it now."** ²⁸None of those around the table realized what was happening. ²⁹Some thought that Judas, their trusted treasurer, was being told to go buy what was needed for the Passover celebration, or perhaps to go give something to the poor. ³⁰So Judas left quickly and went out into the dark night to betray Jesus.

Jesus Predicts Peter's Denial

³¹After Judas left the room, Jesus said, **"The time has come for the glory of God to surround the Son of Man, and God will be greatly glorified**

---

a 13:21 As translated from the Greek. The Aramaic describes Jesus' emotion as "feeling a profound tenderness," or "his spirit felt a longing." We can conclude that everything within our Lord Jesus was moved deeply by the thought of being betrayed by one of his beloved disciples.

b 13:23 The Aramaic is, "the one Jesus showed mercy to." This was obviously John, the one who wrote this gospel. Remember, you too can say, "I am the disciple who Jesus dearly loves and shows mercy to."

c 13:23 This could be a figure of speech for "the place of honor."

d 13:26 This was culturally an act of cherished friendship and intimacy, to hand over choice bits of food to a friend. This is the love of Christ, to give food to his enemy. It is no wonder Satan entered his heart after Judas ate the bread handed to him by his friend. For how can one accept the gift of true friendship and still hold on to treachery and the spirit of betrayal?

e 13:27 This is an Aramaic word that means "adversary."

through what happens to me.[a] [32]And very soon God will unveil the glory of the Son of Man.[b]

[33]"My dear friends,[c] I only have a brief time left to be with you. And then you will search and long for me. But I tell you what I told the Jewish leaders: you'll not be able to come where I am.[d]

[34]"So I give you now a new[e] commandment: Love each other just as much as I have loved you. [35]For when you demonstrate the same love I have for you by loving one another, everyone will know that you're my true followers."

[36]Peter the Rock interjected, "But, Master, where are you going?"

Jesus replied, **"Where I am going you won't be able to follow, but one day you will follow me there."**

[37]Peter the Rock[f] said, "What do you mean I'm not able to follow you now? I would sacrifice my life to die for you!"[g]

[38]Jesus answered, **"Would you really lay down your life for me, Peter? Here's the absolute truth: Before the rooster crows in the morning, you will say three times that you don't even know me!"[h]**

---

a 13:31 Or "The Son of Man was glorified and the Father was glorified by him."

b 13:32 Or "Since God is glorified in him (the Son of Man) God will also glorify him in himself, and glorify him immediately." The Greek text has the word *doxazo* (glory or honor) five times in verses 31–32. This repetition would mean that it speaks of more than simply honor. It is the clear statement of the exchange of glory between God and his Son, Jesus Christ.

c 13:33 Or "children."

d 13:33 See John 7:33–34.

e 13:34 Jesus sets a new standard of love before his followers. Although the Old Testament does instruct us to love one another (Leviticus 19:18, 34 and Deuteronomy 10:18), Jesus now gives the commandment to use his standard of love for us as the true measurement of love as we care for one another.

f 13:37 The Aramaic is translated, "Simon the Rock."

g 13:37 The Aramaic uses the word "consecrate," which means to offer up a sacrifice. Peter implies that he would willingly offer himself in Jesus' place.

h 13:38 Peter, like all of us, resisted the acknowledgment of his weakness and chose to cling to the illusion of strength. Peter was given the sign of a rooster crowing, for that is what he was. He was like a crowing rooster, strutting in pride. "Rocky" got cocky and forgot where true strength is found.

Fourteen

Jesus Comforts His Disciples

[1]"Don't worry or surrender to your fear.[a] For you've believed in God, now trust and believe in me also.[b] [2]My Father's house has many dwelling places.[c] If it were otherwise, I would tell you plainly, because I go[d] to prepare a place for you to rest. [3]And when everything is ready, I will come back and take[e] you to myself so that you will be where I am. [4]And you already know the way to the place where I'm going."[f]

[5]Thomas said to him, "Master, we don't know where you're going, so how could we know the way there?"

[6]Jesus explained, "I am the Way, I am the Truth,[g] and I am the Life. No one comes next to the Father[h] except through *union with me.*[i] To know me is to know my Father too. [7]And from now on you will realize that you have seen him and experienced him."

---

a 14:1 Or "Don't let your hearts be distressed." The Aramaic is translated, "Let not your heart flutter."

b 14:1 Or "Believe in God and believe in me."

c 14:2 Or "There are many resting places on the way to my Father's house." Or "There are many homes in my Father's household." The Father's house is also mentioned by Jesus in John 2:16, where it is his temple on earth, his dwelling place. This is not just heaven, but the dwelling place of God among men. There is ample room for people from every nation and ethnicity, room to spare, for the Church, the Body of Christ, is now the House of God. See 1 Timothy 3:15, 1 Corinthians 3:16, Hebrews 3:6, Ephesians 2:21–22, and 1 Peter 2:5. Every believer is now one of the many dwelling places that make up God's house (temple). See also verse 23.

d 14:2 Jesus' "going" was to go through death and resurrection in order to make us ready to be his dwelling place. He had to "go," not to heaven, but to the cross and pass through resurrection.

e 14:3 The Greek verb used here, *paralambano*, is the word used for a bridegroom coming to take his bride. He "takes" us as his bride through his death and resurrection. His "coming back" can also refer to his "coming" to live within believers.

f 14:4 Or "You know where I'm going and the way to get there."

g 14:6 Or "the True Reality."

h 14:6 Jesus does more than take us to heaven, he brings us next to (alongside of) the Father. The Father is the destination.

i 14:6 Or "through (faith in) me."

[8]Philip spoke up, "Lord, show us the Father, and that will be all that we need!"

[9]Jesus replied, **"Philip, I've been with you all this time and you still don't know who I am? How could you ask me to show you the Father, for anyone who has looked at me has seen the Father. [10]Don't you believe that the Father is living in me and that I am living in the Father? Even my words are not my own but come from my Father, for he lives in me and performs his miracles of power through me. [11]Believe that I live as one with my Father and that my Father lives as one with me—or at least, believe because of the mighty miracles I have done.**

[12]**"I tell you this timeless truth: The person who follows me in faith, believing in me, will do the same mighty miracles that I do—even greater miracles than these because I go to be with my Father! [13]For I will do whatever you ask me to do when you ask me in my name. And that is how the Son will show what the Father is really like and bring glory to him. [14]Ask me anything in my name, and I will do it for you!"**

Jesus Prophesies about the Holy Spirit

[15]**"Loving me empowers you to obey my commands.**[a] [16-17]**And I will ask the Father and he will give you another**[b] **Savior,**[c] **the Holy Spirit of Truth, who will be to you a friend just like me—and he will never leave you. The world won't receive him because they can't see him or know him. But you**

---

a 14:15 Love for Christ is proven and demonstrated by our obedience to all that he says.

b 14:16 The Greek word *allos* means "another of the same kind." As Jesus is the Savior from the guilt of sin, the Holy Spirit is the Savior who saves us from the power of sin by living through us in fullness.

c 14:16 The Greek word used here is *paráklētos*, a technical word that could be translated "defense attorney." It means, "one called to stand next to you as a helper." Various translations have rendered this, "Counselor, Comforter, Advocate, Encourager, Intercessor, or Helper." However none of these words alone are adequate and fall short in explaining the full meaning. The translator has chosen the word *Savior*, for it depicts the role of the Holy Spirit to protect, defend, and save us from our self and our enemies and keep us whole and healed. He is the One who guides and defends, comforts and consoles. Keep in mind that the Holy Spirit is the Spirit of Christ, our Savior. The Aramaic word is *paraqleta*, which is taken from two root words: 1) *praq*, "to end, finish, or to save," and 2) *lyta*, which means "the curse." What a beautiful word picture, the Holy Spirit comes to end the work of the curse (of sin) in our lives and to save us from its every effect! *Paraqleta* means "a redeemer who ends the curse." See Strong's entries 6561 and 6562; A Compendious Syriac Dictionary, p. 237; and Oraham's Dictionary, p. 250.

will know him intimately, because he will make his home in you and will live inside you.[a]

[18]"I promise that I will never leave you helpless or abandon you as orphans—I will come back to you![b] [19]Soon I will leave this world and they will see me no longer, but you will see me, because I will live again, and you will come alive too. [20]So when that day comes, you will know that I am living in the Father and that you are one with me, for I will be living in you. [21]Those who truly love me are those who obey my commandments. Whoever passionately loves me will be passionately loved by my Father. And I will passionately love you in return and will manifest my life within you."

[22]Then one of the disciples named Judas[c] (not Judas Iscariot) said, "Lord, why is it you will only reveal your identity to us and not to everyone?"

[23]Jesus replied, "Loving me empowers you to obey my word.[d] And my Father will love you so deeply that we will come to you and make you our dwelling place. [24]But those who don't love me will not obey my words. The Father did not send me to speak my own revelation, but the words of my Father. [25]I am telling you this while I am still with you. [26]But when the Father sends the Spirit of Holiness, the One like me who sets you free,[e] he will teach you all things in my name. And he will inspire you to remember every word that I've told you.

[27]"I leave the gift of peace with you—my peace. Not the kind of fragile peace given by the world, but my perfect peace. Don't yield to fear or be troubled in your hearts—instead, be courageous![f] [28]"Remember

---

a 14:17 Jesus is prophesying about the coming of the Holy Spirit at Pentecost, who will indwell every believer. See Acts 2.

b 14:18 There are three ways Jesus will come to them. He came after his resurrection and appeared numerous times to his disciples. He came in the person of the Holy Spirit at Pentecost to live within them (Romans 8:9) and he will come in the *parousia,* known traditionally as the second coming.

c 14:22 Judas was a common name in the time of Jesus. It is actually the name Judah.

d 14:23 Love for Christ is proven and demonstrated by our obedience to all that he says.

e 14:26 The Aramaic is translated, "the Redeemer from the curse." See footnote on 14:16.

f 14:27 These are the same words Moses gave before he died and the words God spoke to Joshua as he entered into his life's plan of taking the Promised Land for Israel. See Deuteronomy 31:8 and

what I've told you, that I must go away, but I promise to come back to you. So if you truly love me, you will be glad for me, since I'm returning to my Father, who is greater than I. [29]So when all of these things happen, you will still trust and cling to me. [30]I won't speak with you much longer, for the ruler of this dark world is coming. But he has no power over me, *for he has nothing to use against me.*[a] [31]I am doing exactly what the Father destined for me to accomplish,[b] so that the world will discover how much I love my Father. Now come with me."

Jesus the Living Vine

[1]"I am a true sprouting vine, and the farmer who tends the vine is my Father. [2]He cares for the branches connected to me by lifting and propping up the fruitless branches[c] and pruning[d] every fruitful branch to yield a greater harvest. [3]The words I have spoken over you have already cleansed[e] you. [4]So you must remain in life-union with me,[f] for I remain in life-union with you. For as a branch severed from the vine will not bear

Joshua 1:8–9 and 10:25. God has not given us a spirit of cowardly fear. See also 2 Timothy 1:7.

a 14:30 Implied in the text and in the word "devil," which means slanderer and accuser.

b 14:31 Or "commanded me to do."

c 15:2 The Greek phrase can also be translated, "he takes up (to himself) every fruitless branch." He doesn't remove these branches, but he takes them to himself. As the wise and loving farmer, he lifts them up off the ground to enhance their growth. In the context, Christ's endless love for his disciples on the last night of his life on earth seems to emphasize God's love even for those who fail and disappoint him. Peter's denial didn't bring rejection from Jesus.

d 15:2 The Greek word for pruning, *kathairo,* can also mean cleansing.

e 15:3 Or "pruned."

f 15:4 Or "grafted into me."

fruit, so your life will be fruitless unless you live your life intimately joined to mine.

⁵"I am the sprouting vine and you're my branches.ᵃ As you live in union with me as your source, fruitfulness will stream from within you—but when you live separated from me you are powerless. ⁶If a person is separated from me, he is discarded; such branches are gathered up and thrown into the fire to be burned. ⁷But if you live in life-union with me and if my wordsᵇ live powerfullyᶜ within you—then you can ask whatever you desire and it will be done. ⁸When your lives bear abundant fruit, you demonstrate that you are my mature disciples who glorify my Father!

⁹"I love each of you with the same love that the Father loves me. You must continually let my love nourish your hearts. ¹⁰If you keep my commands, you will live in my love, just as I have kept my Father's commands, for I continually live nourished and empowered by his love. ¹¹My purpose for telling you these things is so that the joy that I experience will fill your hearts with overflowing gladness!

¹²"So this is my command: Love each other deeply, as much as I have loved you.ᵈ ¹³For the greatest love of all is a love that sacrifices all. And this great love is demonstrated when a person sacrifices his lifeᵉ for his friends.

¹⁴"You show that you are my intimate friends when you obeyᶠ allᵍ that I command you. ¹⁵I have never called you 'servants,'ʰ because

---

a 15:5 See Isaiah 4:2, 11:1–2, and Revelation 1:20. The branch of the Lord is now Christ living in his people, branching out through them. The church is now his lampstand with seven branches.

b 15:7 This is the Greek word *rhema*, which refers to the spoken words, or the sayings, of God.

c 15:7 The Aramaic is translated, "my words take hold (are strong) within you."

d 15:12 Because we are all branches in one vine, if we don't love one another it means that our fellowship with the vine has been cut off. To bear fruit must come from loving each other, for the same Christ-life lives within every believer. We are not branches of many trees, but of one vine.

e 15:13 Or "willingly lay down his soul for his friends." The Aramaic word for "friends" is actually "family," or "relatives."

f 15:14 The Greek verb indicates, "if you keep on obeying as a habit."

g 15:14 The Aramaic is translated, "all;" the Greek is translated, "what I command you."

h 15:15 As translated from the Aramaic. The Greek is, "I will no longer call you servants." The Greek

a master doesn't confide in his servants, and servants don't always understand what the master is doing. But I call you my most intimate friends,[a] for I reveal to you everything that I've heard from my Father. [16]You didn't choose me, but I've chosen[b] and commissioned you to go into the world[c] to bear fruit. And your fruit will last, because whatever you ask of my Father, for my sake,[d] he will give it to you! [17]So this is my parting command: Love one another deeply!

True Disciples Can Expect Persecution

[18]"Just remember, when the unbelieving world hates you, they first hated me. [19]If you were to give your allegiance to the world, they would love and welcome you as one of their own. But because you won't align yourself with the values of this world, they will hate you. I have chosen you and taken you out of the world to be mine. [20]So remember what I taught you, that a servant isn't superior to his master.[e] And since they persecuted me, they will also persecute you. And if they obey my teachings, they will also obey yours. [21]They will treat you this way because you are mine,[f] and they don't know the One who sent me.

[22]"If I had not come and revealed myself[g] to the unbelieving world, they would not feel the guilt of their sin, but now their sin is left uncovered.[h] [23]If anyone hates me, they hate my Father also. [24]If I had not performed miracles in their presence like no one else has done, they would not feel the guilt of their sins. But now, they have seen and hated

---

word for servants is *doulos,* which means "slaves."

a 15:15 Both the Aramaic and Greek word for "intimate friends" is actually "those cared for from the womb." You are more than a friend to him, for you were born again from his wounded side.

b 15:16 The Aramaic is, "I have invited you (as dinner guests)."

c 15:16 This could mean "to go on into maturity (character)," or "to go into the world (ministry)." However, the "choosing" and "commissioning" infers the latter.

d 15:16 Or "in my name."

e 15:20 Or "Redeemer." See John 13:16.

f 15:21 Or "because of my name."

g 15:22 As translated from the Aramaic. The Greek is, "spoken these things."

h 15:22 As translated from the Aramaic.

both me and my Father. ²⁵And all of this has happened to fulfill what is written in their Scriptures:^a

They hated me for no reason.^b

²⁶"And I will send you the Divine Encourager^c from the very presence of my Father. He will come to you, the Spirit of Truth, emanating from the Father, and he will speak^d to you about me. ²⁷And you will tell everyone the truth about me, for you have walked with me from the start."

Sixteen

Jesus Warns His Disciples

¹"I have told you this so that you would not surrender to confusion or doubt.^e ²For you will be excommunicated from the synagogues, and a time is coming when you will be put to death by misguided ones who will presume to be doing God a great service by putting you to death.^f ³And they will do these things because they don't know anything about the Father or me. ⁴I'm telling you this now so that when their time comes you will remember that I foretold it. I didn't tell you this in the beginning because I was still with you. ⁵But now that I'm about to leave you and go back to join the One who sent me, you need to be told. Yet, not one of

---

a 15:25 Or "written in their law."

b 15:24 See Psalm 35:19 and 69:4. The Greek text can also be translated, "They hated my undeserved gifts."

c 15:26 Or "Redeemer from the curse." See footnote on 14:16.

d 15:26 Or "provide evidence."

e 16:1 Or "so that you won't have a trap laid for you." The Aramaic is translated, "so that you will not be crushed."

f 16:2 The Aramaic is, "those who kill you will think they are presenting a holy offering to God."

you are asking me where I'm going. [6]Instead your hearts are filled with sadness because I've told you these things. [7]But here's the truth: it's to your advantage that I go away, for if I don't go away the Divine Encourager[a] will not be released to you. But after I depart, I will send him to you. [8]And when he comes, he will expose sin and prove that the world is wrong about God's righteousness and his judgments.

[9]"'Sin,' because they refuse to believe in who I am.

[10]"God's 'righteousness,' because I'm going back to join the Father and you'll see me no longer.

[11]"And 'judgment' because the ruler of this dark world has already received his sentence.[b]

[12]"There is so much more I would like to say to you, but it's more than you can grasp at this moment. [13]But when the truth-giving Spirit comes, he will unveil the reality of every truth[c] within you. He won't speak his own message, but only what he hears from the Father, and he will reveal prophetically to you what is to come. [14]He will glorify me on the earth, for he will receive from me what is mine[d] and reveal it to you. [15]Everything that belongs to the Father belongs to me—that's why I say that the Divine Encourager will receive what is mine and reveal it to you. [16]Soon you won't see me any longer, but then, after a little while, you will see me *in a new way.*"[e]

[17]Some of the disciples asked each other, "What does he mean, 'Soon you won't see me,' and, 'A little while after that and you will see me in a new way'? And what does he mean, 'Because I'm going to my

---

a 16:7 Or "the Redeemer of the curse." See footnote on John 14:16.

b 16:11 In essence, "sin . . . righteousness . . . and judgment are related to three persons." Sin is related to Adam, for it was through Adam that sin entered humanity (Romans 5:12). Righteousness is related to Christ, because it comes through him, and he has become our righteousness (1 Corinthians 1:30). Judgment is related to Satan, for the pure works of Christ bring judgment to the works of Satan. If we do not embrace Christ's righteousness, we will share Satan's judgment.

c 16:13 The Greek word for truth is "reality," not doctrine. It is the application of truth that matters, not just a superficial knowledge.

d 16:14 As translated from the Aramaic. Or "he plants what is mine and shows it to you."

e 16:16 Jesus uses two different Greek words for *see* in this verse. The Aramaic adds, "because I go to my Father."

Father'?" ¹⁸So they kept on repeating, "What's the meaning of 'a little while'? We have no clue what he's talking about!"

¹⁹Jesus knew what they were thinking, and it was obvious that they were anxious to ask him what he had meant,ᵃ so he spoke up and said, ²⁰"Let me make it quite clear: you will weep and be over-come with grief *over what happens to me.* The unbelieving world will be happy, while you will be filled with sorrow. But know this, your sadness will turn into joy *when you see me again!* ²¹Just like a woman giving birth experiences intense labor pains in delivering her baby,ᵇ yet after the child is born she quickly forgets what she went through because of the overwhelming joy of knowing that a new baby has been born into the world.

²²"So will you also pass through a time of intense sorrow *when I am taken from you,* but you will see me again! And then your hearts will burst with joy, with no one being able to take it from you!ᶜ ²³For here is eternal truth: When that time comes you won't need to ask me for anything, but instead you will go directly to the Father and ask him for anything you desire and he will give it to you, because of your rela-tionship with me.ᵈ ²⁴Until now you've not been bold enough to ask the Father for a single thing in my name,ᵉ but now you can ask, and keep on asking him! And you can be sure that you'll receive what you ask for, and your joy will have no limits!

---

a 16:19 Or "Are you asking each other what I meant when I told you, 'A little while and you will see me no more, and then after a little while you will see me'?"

b 16:21 Or "because her time (for delivery) has come." It is fascinating that Jesus speaks of the disciples in the terms of giving birth. Christ is being formed within us (Galatians 4:19). The church continues in "labor" today so that Jesus can be seen again through us. See Revelation 12:1–5.

c 16:22 Jesus is referring to the prophecy of Isaiah 66:7 and 14.

d 16:23 Or "he will give it to you in my name."

e 16:24 To ask in Jesus' name is to ask in the name of "I Am." We take all the fullness of Jesus (his name, his glory, his virtue) as the "I Am" of Exodus 3:14—because of our relationship with him.

²⁵"I have spoken to you using figurative language,ᵃ but the time is coming when I will no longer teach you with veiled speech, but I will teach you about the Father with your eyes unveiled.ᵇ ²⁶And I will not need to ask the Father on your behalf, for you'll ask him directly because of your new relationship with me.ᶜ ²⁷For the Father tenderly loves you, because you love me and believe that I've come from God. ²⁸I came to you sent from the Father's presence, and I entered into the created world, and now I will leave this world and return to the Father's side."

²⁹His disciples said, "At last you're speaking to us clearly and not using veiled speech and metaphors! ³⁰Now we understand that you know everything there is to know, and we don't need to question you further. And everything you've taught us convinces us that you have come directly from God!"

³¹Jesus replied, "Now you finally believe in me. ³²And the time has come when you will all be scattered, and each one of you will go your own way, leaving me alone!ᵈ Yet I am never alone, for the Father is always with me. ³³And everything I've taught you is so that the peace which is in me will be in you and will give you great confidence as you rest in me. For in this unbelieving world you will experience trouble and sorrows, but you must be courageous,ᵉ for I have conquered the world!"ᶠ

---

a 16:25 This is the Greek word, *paroimiais,* which can mean obscure figurative speech, analogies, parables, proverbs, metaphors, or allegory. These were all utilized as Jesus' preferred teaching method while on earth. See Matthew 13:34 and John 16:29.

b 16:25 As translated from the Aramaic.

c 16:26 Or "in my name."

d 16:32 This will fulfill the prophecy of Zechariah 13:7.

e 16:33 Or "cheer up!"

f 16:33 Jesus has taken away the power this world has to defeat us and has conquered it for us. Peace is resting in his victory.

Seventeen

Jesus Finished the Father's Work

¹This is what Jesus prayed as he looked up into heaven,
"Father, the time has come.
>Unveil the glorious splendor of your Son[a]
>so that I will magnify your glory!
²You have already given me authority[b] over all people so that I may give
>the gift of eternal life to all those that you have given to me.
³Eternal life means to know and experience you as the only true God,[c]
>and to know and experience Jesus Christ, as the Son whom you have sent.
⁴I have glorified you on the earth
>by faithfully doing everything you've told me to do.
⁵So my Father, restore me back to the glory
>that we shared together when we were face to face
>before the universe was created."[d]

Jesus Prays for His Disciples

⁶"Father, I have manifested who you really are
>and I have revealed you[e] to the men and women that you gave to

---

a 17:1 Or "Glorify your Son!" The Father unveiled the glory of his Son on the cross, by the empty tomb, through his ascension into heaven, and by the mighty outpouring of the Holy Spirit upon his church.

b 17:2 The Aramaic is translated, "responsibility."

c 17:3 The Aramaic is translated, "the God of Truth." This alludes to Deuteronomy 6:4.

d 17:5 The Aramaic is translated, "before the light of the universe."

e 17:6 Or "I have made known your name." The Greek word, phaneroo, means, "to make visible," "to manifest," "to reveal," and "to be plainly recognized." See Strong's concordance #5319.

me.[a] They were yours, and you gave them to me,
and they have fastened your Word firmly to their hearts.
⁷And now at last they know that everything I have is a gift from you,
⁸And the very words you gave to me to speak I have passed on to them.
They have received your words and *carry them in their hearts.*
They are convinced that I have come from your presence,
and they have fully believed that you sent me to represent you.
⁹So with deep love,[b] I pray for my disciples.
I'm not asking on behalf of the unbelieving world,[c]
but for those who belong to you, those you have given me.
¹⁰For all who belong to me now belong to you.
And all who belong to you now belong to me as well,
and my glory is revealed through *their surrendered lives.*[d]
¹¹"Holy Father, I am about to leave this world[e]
to return and be with you, but my disciples will remain here.
So I ask that by the power of your name
protect each one that you have given me, and watch over them
so that they will be united as one, even as we are one.
¹²While I was with these that you have given me,[f]
I have kept them safe by the your name that you have given me.
Not one of them is lost, except the one that was destined to be lost,[g]
so that the Scripture would be fulfilled.

---

a 17: Or "You gave to me out of the world."

b 17:9 The Aramaic can be translated, "I desired (loved) them." The Greek is, "I pray for them." The translator has chosen to include both concepts.

c 17:9 This is emphatic in the Greek sentence structure. How could it be that Jesus loves the world and gave himself for the sin of the world, yet emphasizes that he is praying for his disciples and not praying for the world? Jesus' coming into the world brings life to those who believe and judgment to those who do not. The implication is that the key to reaching the world is the life, maturity, unity, and love of the disciples. This does not mean that Jesus doesn't love the world, but that the world will only be reached when the disciples come into the fullness of Christ and in unity of the faith. This is what consumes the heart of Jesus as he prays for them before the cross.

d 17:10 Or "I am glorified in them."

e 17:11 Or "I am no longer in the world."

f 17:12 See footnote on verse 11.

g 17:12 Or "son of perdition," which is a Semitic idiom that means, "to be destined to destruction." This obviously refers to Judas, the betrayer. See also Psalm 41:9 and John 6:70.

¹³"But now I am returning to you so Father,
   I pray[a] that they will experience and enter into my joyous delight
   in you[b]
   so that it is fulfilled in them and overflows.
¹⁴I have given them your message
   and that is why the unbelieving world hates them.
   For their allegiance is no longer to this world
   because I am not of this world.
¹⁵I am not asking that you remove them from the world,
   but I ask that you guard their hearts from evil,[c]
¹⁶For they no longer belong to this world any more than I do.
¹⁷"Your Word is truth! So make them holy by the truth.
¹⁸I have commissioned them to represent me
   just as you commissioned me to represent you.
¹⁹And now I dedicate myself to them as a holy sacrifice
   so that they will live as fully dedicated to God
   and be made holy by your truth.[d]

Jesus Prays for You

²⁰"And I ask not only for these disciples,
   but also for all those who will one day
   believe in me through their message.
²¹I pray for them all to be joined together as one[e]
   even as you and I, Father, are joined together as one.
   I pray for them to become one with us[f]
   so that the world will recognize that you sent me.

---

a 17:13 Or "I speak these things (this prayer) in the world (before I leave)."

b 17:13 This "delight" is more than happiness. It is the complete satisfaction that comes in knowing that our lives are pleasing to the Father and that we fulfill his desires on the earth. This is the delight that Jesus shares with us and prays that we would experience.

c 17:15 Or "the evil one (Satan)." The implication is that the disciples of Jesus will influence the systems of this world but need to be preserved from evil influences.

d 17:19 The Aramaic can be translated, "And in their sight I will glorify (consecrate) myself, so that they will be glorified (consecrated) by the truth."

e 17:21 Jesus prayed for the birth of the church, made up of Jewish and non-Jewish believers.

f 17:21 Or "in us."

²²For the very glory you have given to me I have given them
    so that they will be joined together as one
    and experience the same unity that we enjoy.ᵃ
²³You live fully in me and now I live fully in them
    so that they will experience perfect unity,ᵇ
    and the world will be convinced that you have sent me,
    for they will see that you love each one of them
    with the same passionate love that you have for me.
²⁴"Father, I ask that you allow everyone that you have given to me,
    to be with me where I am!ᶜ
    Then they will see my full glory—
    the very splendor you have placed upon me
    because you have loved me even before the beginning of time.
²⁵"You are my righteous Father,ᵈ
    but the unbelieving world has never known you
    in the perfect way that I know you! *And all those who believe in*
    *me*ᵉ *also know that you have sent me!*
²⁶I have revealed to them who you areᶠ
    and I will continue to make you even more real to them,
    so that they may experience the same endless love
    that you have for me,
    for your love will now live in them, even as I live in them!"

---

a 17:22 It is important to note that the key to unity among believers is experiencing the glory of God that Jesus has imparted to us. As one with God through faith in Christ, he shares his glory with us, since we are not "another," but have been made one with the Triune God through the blood of Jesus. See Isaiah 42:8.

b 17:23 The Aramaic is, "shrink into one." When we see Jesus in one another, our vaulted opinions of ourselves will shrink.

c 17:24 This is experienced not only after we die, but also took place when the ascended Christ took us up into the heavenly realm and seated us at his side with the Father. See Ephesians 2:6 and Colossians 3:1–4.

d 17:25 As translated from the Aramaic.

e 17:25 The Greek is simply, "these (disciples)."

f 17:26 Or "I have revealed your name to them."

Eighteen

Jesus in the Garden of Gethsemane

[1]After Jesus finished this prayer; he left with his disciples and went across the Kidron Valley[a] to a place where there was a garden.[b] [2]Judas, the traitor, knew where this place was, for Jesus had gone there often with his disciples. [3]The Pharisees and the leading priests had given Judas a large detachment[c] of Roman soldiers and temple police to seize Jesus. Judas guided them to the garden, all of them carrying torches and lanterns and armed *with swords and spears.*[d] [4]Jesus, knowing full well what was about to happen, went out to the garden entrance to meet them. Stepping forward, he asked, **"Who are you looking for?"**

[5]"Jesus of Nazareth,"[e] they replied. (Now Judas, the traitor, was among them.)

He replied, **"I Am he."**

[6]And the moment Jesus spoke the words, **"I Am he,"** the mob fell backward to the ground![f]

---

a 18:1 The Kidron ravine is the path David took when he was forced to flee Jerusalem because of the betrayal of his son Absalom. David went up the Mount of Olives weeping. Jesus went up also in sorrow. David went up to save himself; Jesus went up to save the people of the world.

b 18:1 This is the Garden of Gethsemane, which means "olive press." Jesus not only went to the garden to pray, but to be captured. He knew full well the Father's plan. Just as Adam fell in a garden of paradise, Jesus stood faithful in a garden of betrayal.

c 18:3 The Greek and Aramaic word used for this company of soldiers implies quite a large number, up to 500 to 600 men sent to arrest Jesus. Even his enemies knew his power was great.

d 18:3 The Greek word is, "foot-soldiers' weapons."

e 18:5 Or "Jesus, the Nazarene." This is the Aramaic word *nussraya*, which means "victorious one," or "heir of a powerful family." The Hebrew word for "Nazareth" comes from the root word *netzer*, which means "branch." See Isaiah 4:2 and 11:1.

f 18:5 This was a stunning event as the great I Am spoke his name before those who sought to seize him. It is obvious in the text that they did not trip over each other in surprise, for every one of these strong men fell backward to the ground by the power of God. Jesus was in charge that night as the Captain of the Host of the Lord. They could not seize him unless he permitted them to do so. What a wonderful Savior who willingly submitted to the hands of cruel men to bring us the gift of salvation.

⁷So once more, Jesus asked them, **"Who are you looking for?"**

As they stood up, they answered, "Jesus of Nazareth."

⁸Jesus replied, **"I told you that I Am the one you're looking for, so if you want me, let these men go home."**ᵃ

⁹He said this to fulfill the prophecy he had spoken, **"Father, not one of those you have given me has been lost."**ᵇ

¹⁰Suddenly, Peter the Rock took out his sword and struck the high priest's servant, slashing off his right ear!ᶜ The servant's name was Malchus.ᵈ

¹¹Jesus ordered Peter, **"Put your sword away! Do you really think I will avoid the suffering**ᵉ **which my Father has assigned to me?"**

Jesus Is Taken Before Annas

¹²Then the soldiers and their captain, along with the Jewish officers, seized Jesus and tied him up. ¹³They took him first to Annas,ᶠ as he was the father-in-law of Caiaphas, the high priest that year.ᵍ ¹⁴Caiaphas was the one who had persuaded the Jewish leaders that it would be better off to have one person die for the sake of the people.ʰ

Peter's First Denial

¹⁵Peter the Rock and another disciple followed along behind them as they took Jesus into the courtyard of Annas' palace. Since the other disciple was

---

a 18:8 "These men" were the eleven disciples who were with Jesus in the garden.

b 18:9 See John 6:39 and 17:12.

c 18:10 This event is a vivid picture of what happens when we act impetuously and in anger. We hinder people's ability to hear our message (we cut off their ear) when we walk in angry offense toward others.

d 18:10 Malchus' name means "king." Perhaps at the moment of healing his ear, Jesus personally revealed himself to Malchus in a supernatural way, the King who healed a king. Jesus is the true servant to the High Priest. We can imagine Jesus reaching out his hand to help Malchus up. And in an instant, Malchus believes. Malchus' ears, both of them, are healed.

e 18:11 Or "Shall I not drink the cup (of suffering) assigned me by the Father?"

f 18:13 John is the only gospel account that inserts this pre-trial meeting with Annas. He was the retired and illegal high priest.

g 18:13 Or "close friend to the high priest." The priesthood was corrupt in the time of Jesus. It was not proper for two men to hold the office of high priest at the same time, as it apparently was done in Jesus' day. They both were called high priest in this narrative. See John 18:19, 24.

h 18:14 See John 11:49–51.

well known to the high priest, he entered in,[a] [16]but Peter was left standing outside by the gate. Then the other disciple came back out to the servant girl who was guarding the gate and convinced her to allow Peter the Rock inside. [17]As he passed inside, the young servant girl guarding the gate took a look at Peter and said to him, "Aren't you one of his disciples?"

He denied it, saying, "No! I'm not!"

[18]Now because it was cold, the soldiers and guards made a charcoal fire and were standing around it to keep warm. So Peter huddled there with them around the fire.

Jesus Interrogated by Annas

[19]The high priest interrogated Jesus concerning his disciples[b] and his teachings.

[20]Jesus answered Annas' questions by saying, **"I have said nothing in secret. At all times I have taught openly and publicly in a synagogue, in the temple courts, and wherever the people assemble. [21]Why would you ask me for evidence to condemn me? Ask those who have heard what I've taught. They can tell you."**

[22]Just then one of the guards standing near Jesus punched him in the face with his fist[c] and said, "How dare you answer the high priest like that!"

[23]Jesus replied, **"If my words are evil, then prove it. But if I haven't broken any laws, then why would you hit me?"**

[24]Then Annas sent Jesus, still tied up, across the way to the high priest Caiaphas.

---

a 18:15 Although it is impossible to determine who exactly was this other disciple, some have surmised it was John himself, or Nicodemus. If it was Nicodemus, as a leader among the Pharisees, this would explain his inclusion into the proceedings taking place that night.

b 18:19 It is interesting that Annas was concerned about Jesus' disciples. The religious spirit is always concerned with impressive numbers and influence. Jesus only had twelve disciples who were always with him.

c 18:22 The Greek is simply, "struck him." This could have been with a rod, for the verb has an etymological connection to the word for "rod." Most translators have chosen to use, "struck (or slapped) with his hand." Regardless, Jesus was beaten everywhere he went that night and the next morning until he was finally crucified.

Peter's Second and Third Denial

²⁵Meanwhile, Peter the Rock was still standing in the courtyard by the fire. And one of the guards standing there said to him, "Aren't you one of his disciples? I know you are!" Peter swore[a] and said, "I am not his disciple!" ²⁶But one of the servants of the high priest, a relative to the man whose ear Peter the Rock had cut off, looked at him and said, "Wait! Didn't I see you out there in the garden with Jesus?" ²⁷Then Peter the Rock denied it the third time and said, "No!"—and at that very same moment, a rooster crowed nearby.

Jesus Interrogated by Pilate

²⁸Before dawn they took Jesus from his trial before Caiaphas to the Roman governor's palace.[b] Now the Jews refused to go into the Roman governor's residence to avoid ceremonial defilement before eating the Passover meal. ²⁹So Pilate came outside where they waited and asked them pointedly, "Tell me, what exactly is the accusation[c] that you bring against this man? What has he done?"

³⁰They answered, "We wouldn't be coming here to hand over[d] this 'criminal' to you if he wasn't guilty of some wrongdoing!"

³¹Pilate said, "Very well, then you take him yourselves and go pass judgment on him according to your Jewish laws!"

But the Jewish leaders complained and said, "We don't have legal authority to put anyone to death. *You should have him crucified!*"[e] ³²(This was to fulfill the words of Jesus when he predicted the manner of death that he would die.)

---

a 18:25 As translated from the Aramaic. This is a very strong word that can also be translated, "blasphemed." God's loving grace forgave Peter's sin—and our sin.

b 18:28 The Greek is *Praetorium*, which is the transliteration of the Latin word meaning "general's tent." It became used for the Roman governor's official residence.

c 18:29 The Aramaic word for "accusation" is similar to the word *devil* (accuser). Pilate is saying, "What the devil do you have against this man?"

d 18:30 The Aramaic word for "hand over" can also be translated, "betray."

e 18:31 Implied in the context and made explicit to clarify the illegality of the Jews to crucify Jesus. The Jewish law permitted death by stoning, not by crucifixion. The Scriptures had prophesied that he would be pierced and crucified. This was the cruel manner of death used by the Romans to execute the worst of criminals. For this reason they wanted Pilate to order his crucifixion. See John 12:32–34.

Pilate Interrogates Jesus

³³Upon hearing this, Pilate went back inside his palace and summoned Jesus. Looking him over, Pilate asked him, "Are you really the King of the Jews?"

³⁴Jesus replied, *"Are you asking because you really want to know,*^a *or are you only asking this because others have said it about me?"*

³⁵Pilate responded, "Only a Jew would care about this; do I look like a Jew? It's your own people and your religious leaders that have handed you over to me. So tell me, Jesus, what have you done wrong?"

³⁶Jesus looked at Pilate and said, **"The royal power of my kingdom realm doesn't come from this world. If it did, then my followers would be fighting to the end to defend me from the Jewish leaders. My kingdom realm authority is not^b from this realm."^c**

³⁷Then Pilate responded, "Oh, so then you are a king?"

"You are right." Jesus said, **"I was born a King, and I have come into this world to prove what truth really is. And everyone who loves the truth^d will receive my words."**

³⁸Pilate looked at Jesus and said, "What is truth?"^e

As silence filled the room, Pilate went back out to where the Jewish leaders were waiting and said to them, "He's not guilty. I couldn't even find one fault with him.^f ³⁹Now, you do know that we have a custom that I release one prisoner every year at Passover—shall I release your king—the King of the Jews?"^g

---

a 18:34 The Aramaic is, "Have you spoken this from your soul?"

b 18:36 The Aramaic is, "not yet from here."

c 18:36 The Greek text is not, "world," but literally, "this side," or "this realm." The Aramaic word used here can be translated, "not of this age."

d 18:37 Or "everyone who is not deaf to the truth." The Aramaic is, "everyone who came from the truth."

e 18:38 The Aramaic could be translated, "Who is truth?" or, "Who is the true prince?" This skepticism is still voiced today in postmodernism.

f 18:38 As translated from the Aramaic.

g 18:39 Pilate was not a saint. He was considered to be a corrupt and violent leader who would execute people without a trial. (Philo: "De Legatione ad Caium," ed. Mangey, ii.590). He stole money from the temple treasury and brought pagan statues into Jerusalem, which caused riots and death to

⁴⁰They shouted out over and over, "No, not him! Give us Barabbas!"ᵃ (Now Barabbas was a robber and a troublemaker.)

Nineteen

Jesus Is Flogged

¹Then Pilate ordered Jesus to be brutally beaten with a whip of leather straps embedded with metal.ᵇ ²And the soldiers also wove thorn-branches into a crown and set it on his head and placed a purple robe over his shoulders. ³Then, one by one, they came in front of him to mock him by saying, "Hail, to the King of the Jews!" And one after the other, they repeatedly punched him in the face.ᶜ

⁴Once more Pilate went out and said to the Jewish officials, "I will bring him out once more so that you know that I've found nothing wrong with him." ⁵So when Jesus emerged, *bleeding,* wearing the purple robe and the crown of thorns on his head, Pilate said to them, "Look at him! Here is your man!"ᵈ

---

many. It was reported by the church father, Eusebius, ("History Eccl." ii 7) that he was later banished to Vienna in Gaul, where he committed suicide.

a 18:40 Barabbas is an Aramaic name that means "son of the father." He becomes a picture of every son of Adam, our father. Some believe this is a figure of speech, a nickname for one who has no known father, an illegitimate son. Both in Greek and Aramaic, the word for thief or robber can also mean one who leads an insurrection.

b 19:1 This leather whip, embedded with sharpened pieces of bone and metal, was known as "the scorpion." Historians record that many people never survived this cruel flogging. The whips were known to break open the flesh and cut through muscle and sinew all the way to the bone. It was his love for you that enabled him to endure such treatment. For more information on flogging, see www.frugalsites.net/jesus/scourging.htm.

c 19:3 Or "they slapped his faces" (Aramaic). He turned the other cheek and they slapped him on both sides of his face. See Isaiah 53:5–7.

d 19:5 See Zechariah 6:12.

⁶No sooner did the high priests and the temple guards see Jesus that they all shouted in a frenzy, "Crucify him! Crucify him!"

Pilate replied, "You take him then and nail him to a cross yourselves! I told you—he's not guilty! I find no reason to condemn him."

⁷The Jewish leaders shouted back, "But we have the Law! And according to our Law, he must die,ᵃ because he claimed to be the Son of God!"

⁸Then Pilate was greatly alarmedᵇ when he heard that Jesus claimed to be the Son of God! ⁹So he took Jesus back inside and said to him, "Where have you come from?" But once again, silence filled the room. ¹⁰Perplexed, Pilate said, "Are you going to play deaf? Don't you know that I have the power to grant you your freedom or nail you to a tree?"

¹¹Jesus answered, **"You would have no power over me at all, unless it was given to you from above. This is why the one who betrayedᶜ me is guilty of an even greater sin."**

¹²From then on Pilate tried to find a way out of the situation and to set him free, but the Jewish authorities shouted him down: "If you let this man go, you're no friend of Caesar! Anyone who declares himself a king is an enemy of the emperor!"ᵈ

---

a 19:7 They are most likely referring to Leviticus 24:16.

b 19:8 The Aramaic is, "his soul collapsed!"

c 19:11 Or "handed me over." This is the same Greek verb translated "betray" in John 6:71. It would obviously point to Judas. However, some expositors believe it was Caiaphas who handed over Jesus to Pilate, who is referred to here. But in fact, it was the evil spirits of darkness who were controlling Pilate and moving in the hearts of all involved to crucify Jesus. These dark powers would be the ones to experience the tremendous judgment unleashed on them by the power of the cross and resurrection.

d 19:12 In essence, these words were a form of blackmail as the Jewish authorities were reminding Pilate that it would ruin his career if he pardoned Jesus. The term "friends of Caesar" was an honorific title given only to the ruling wealthy class of Romans who would have access to the emperor's court. Many of these "friends of Caesar" were senators and members of the Equestrian Order, known also as the Knights. Pilate's position was a political appointment due to his being a member of this elite class of Romans who took an oath of loyalty to Caesar. They were, in effect, threatening to inform Rome that Pilate was allowing treason in Caesar's empire. As one historian remarked, "One false move and his appointment would be cancelled and his career finished." P. Barnett, *Jesus and the Rise of Early Christianity: A History of New Testament Times,* (Illinois: InterVarsity, 1999), p. 147. This overruled Pilate's desire to set Jesus free. He went on to condemn him to death. To place your career over Jesus is never wise.

¹³So when Pilate heard this threat, he relented and had Jesus, *who was torn and bleeding,* brought outside. Then he went up the elevated stone platform and took his seat on the judgment bench—which in Aramaic is called Gabbatha,^a or "The Bench." ¹⁴And it was now almost noon. And it was the same day they were preparing to slay the Passover lambs.^b

Then Pilate said to the Jewish officials, "Look! Here is your king!"

¹⁵But they screamed out, "Take him away! Take him away and crucify him!"

Pilate replied, "Shall I nail your king to a cross?"

The high priests answered, "We have no other king but Caesar!"

¹⁶Then Pilate handed Jesus over to them. So the soldiers seized him and took him away to be crucified.

Jesus Is Crucified

¹⁷Jesus carried his own cross out of the city to the place called "The Skull," which in Aramaic is Golgotha. ¹⁸And there they nailed him to the cross. He was crucified, along with two others, one on each side with Jesus in the middle. ¹⁹⁻²⁰Pilate had them post a sign over the cross, which was written in three languages—Aramaic, Latin, and Greek. Many of the people of Jerusalem read the sign, for he was crucified near the city. The sign stated: "Jesus of Nazareth, the King of the Jews."^c

---

a 19:13 *Gabbatha* is an Aramaic compound word meaning "on the side of the house" (*gab,* "on the side," and *batha,* "the house"). This would be a stone bench that was used by Pilate to issue sentence. See 2 Chronicles 7:3 and Ezekiel 40:17.

b 19:14 Jesus, our Passover Lamb, would be crucified at the very moment Jewish priests were slaughtering lambs in the temple. See Exodus 12:16. Because there were so many lambs to be killed, the priesthood in that day extended the time of slaughter from noon to twilight—the very hours Jesus was on the cross.

c 19:19–20 Aramaic was the language of the common people in Israel. Hebrew ceased to be their spoken language after 450 BC, after the Jews returned from Babylon. Aramaic remained the language of Israel for nearly one thousand years. Latin was the official language of the Roman empire. The inscription was also in Greek, for the Alexandrian Jews who had come to observe the Passover in Jerusalem would be unable to read Aramaic. The words were, "Jesus, the Nazarene, King of the Jews." The first letters of each of the four words written on the sign in Aramaic (Hebrew) were: Y-H-W-H (*Y'shua Hanozri Wumelech Hayehudim*). To write these letters, YHWH (also known as the Tetragrammaton), was the Hebrew form of writing the sacred name, "Yahweh." No wonder the chief priests were so offended by this sign and insisted that Pilate change it. This was a sign given

²¹But the chief priests of the Jews*ª* said to Pilate, "You must change the sign! Don't let it say, 'King of the Jews,' but rather—'he claimed to be the King of the Jews!'" ²²Pilate responded, "What I have written will remain!"

²³Now when the soldiers crucified Jesus, they divided up his clothes into four shares, one for each of them. But his tunic was seamless, woven from the top to the bottom*ᵇ* as a single garment. ²⁴So the soldiers said to each other, "Don't tear it—let's throw dice*ᶜ* to see who gets it!" The soldiers did all of this not knowing they fulfilled the Scripture that says, "They divided my garments among them and gambled for my garment."*ᵈ*

²⁵Miriam, Jesus' mother, was standing next to his cross, along with Miriam's sister, Miriam the wife of Clopas, and Miriam Magdalene.*ᵉ* ²⁶So when Jesus looked down and saw the disciple he loved standing with her, he said, **"Mother,*ᶠ* look—John*ᵍ* will be a son to you."** ²⁷Then he said, **"John, look—she will be a mother to you!"** From that day on, John accepted Mary into his home *as one of his own family.*ʰ

---

to Israel, for over Jesus' head on the cross was written, Y-H-W-H! God, the Savior, bled to death for you.

a 19:21 There is obvious irony in the Greek text of these two phrases, "King of the Jews" and "the chief priests of the Jews." This is the only place John describes the priests in this way.

b 19:23 The Aramaic could be translated, "his tunic was entirely woven from above." Jesus' tunic was an emblem of his perfect holiness and righteousness as one who came "from above." As believers, we are now robed in that seamless garment of righteousness in Christ.

c 19:24 Or "cast lots." See also verse 25.

d 19:24 See Psalm 22:18.

e 19:25 Many scholars believe that Miriam (Mary)'s sister (Jesus' aunt) was Salome. This would mean she was the wife of Zebedee and the mother of Jacob (James) and John (the writer of the gospel of John). Furthermore, that would mean that Jacob (James) and John were cousins of Jesus. See also Matthew 27:56 and Mark 15:40.

f 19:26 Or "woman."

g 19:26 Although unnamed, this was most certainly John the apostle.

h 19:27 Miriam (Mary) would be nearly fifty years old and a widow. What tenderness we see with Jesus toward his mother! Moments before his death, Jesus thought about Miriam (Mary) and her long journey back to Nazareth and that no one would be there to provide for her. Jesus deeply honored his mother.

Jesus' Death on the Cross

[28]Jesus knew that his mission was accomplished, and to fulfill the Scripture,[a] Jesus said: **"I am thirsty."**

[29]A jar of sour wine was sitting nearby, so they soaked a sponge with it and put it on the stalk of hyssop[b] and raised it to his lips. [30]When he had sipped the sour wine, he said, **"It is finished, my bride!"**[c] Then he bowed his head and surrendered his spirit to God.

[31]The Jewish leaders did not want the bodies of the victims to remain on the cross through the next day, since it was the day of preparation[d] for a very important Sabbath. So they asked Pilate's permission to have the victims' legs broken *to hasten their death*[e] and their bodies taken down before sunset. [32]So the soldiers broke the legs of the two men who were nailed there. [33]But when they came to Jesus, they realized that he had already died, so they decided not to break his legs. [34]But one of the soldiers took a spear and pierced Jesus' side, and blood and water gushed out.[f]

---

a 19:28 See Psalm 22:15 and 69:21. The Fountain of Living Water now *thirsts* for the souls of men and women to come to him. He *thirsts* for your friendship.

b 19:29 The hyssop branch points to the sacrificial death of Jesus. Hyssop is first mentioned in Exodus 12:22 in reference to the application of lamb's blood upon the door posts of the homes of the Hebrews the night of Passover. Hyssop was also used for the cleansing of lepers and points to the cleansing of our souls that happened when Jesus was crucified for sinners (spiritual lepers). See Psalm 51:7 and Hebrews 9:19.

c 19:30 This is from the Aramaic word *kalah*, a homonym that can mean "fulfilled (completed)," and "bride." Jesus finished the work of our salvation for his bride. The translation has combined both concepts. For a fascinating study of the Hebrew word used for "bride" and "finished," with its universe of meaning, see Strong's #3615, 3616, 3617, 3618, and 3634. Although the completed work of salvation was finished on the cross, he continues to work through his church today to extend God's kingdom realm on the earth and glorify the Father through us. He continues to work in us to accomplish all that his cross and resurrection have purchased for us, his bride. His cross fulfilled and finished the prophecies of the Messiah's first coming to the earth. There was nothing written that was not fulfilled and now offered to his bride.

d 19:31 The Aramaic is, "because it was Friday."

e 19:31 Breaking their legs would prevent the one on a cross to lift himself up and take a deep breath. The victim would die sooner by suffocation. The Roman practice was to leave the bodies of the victims on the cross for a day or more as a warning to others. See Deuteronomy 21:22–23.

f 19:34 This becomes a picture of the cleansing by blood and the water of the Holy Spirit. However, water and blood both come forth when a baby is born. Christ gave birth on the cross to "sons." He is the Everlasting Father (Isaiah 9:6), and you must have children to be a Father. We are all born again by the wounded side of Jesus Christ. He not only died for his bride, but he also gave birth to her at the cross.

³⁵(I, John,ᵃ do testify to the certainty of what took place, and I write the truth so that you might also believe.) ³⁶For all these things happened to fulfill the prophecies of the Scriptures:

"Not one of his bones will be broken," ᵇ
³⁷**and, "They will gaze on the one they have pierced!"**ᶜ

Jesus' Burial

³⁸After this, Joseph from the city of Ramah,ᵈ who was a secret disciple of Jesus for fear of the Jewish authorities, asked Pilate if he could remove the body of Jesus. So Pilate granted him permission to remove the body from the cross. ³⁹Now Nicodemus, who had once come to Jesus privately at night, accompanied Joseph, and together they carried a significant amountᵉ of myrrh and aloes to the cross. ⁴⁰Then they took Jesus' body and wrapped it in strips of linen with the embalming spicesᶠ according to the Jewish burial customs. ⁴¹Near the place where Jesus was crucified was a garden, and in the garden there was a new tomb where no one had yet been laid to rest. ⁴²And because the Sabbath was approaching, and the tomb was nearby, that's where they laid the body of Jesus.ᵍ

---

a 19:35 Or "the person who saw this." Although unnamed, it was John, the author of this narrative, who witnessed and testified to the truth of what happened.

b 19:36 See Exodus 12:46 and Psalm 34:20.

c 19:37 See Zechariah 12:10.

d 19:38 As translated from the Aramaic. Or *Arimathea* (Greek), which means, "heights." This was the likely birthplace of the prophet Samuel. Keep in mind that Joseph may have lost a son the age of Jesus when Herod killed all the babies. For fascinating details about Joseph of Arimathea and his supposed encounter with the resurrected Jesus.

e 19:39 Or "approximately one hundred pounds." Some calculate this as Roman pounds weighing thirty kilograms. Others interpret the one hundred pounds to be closer to a liter, or less than one kilogram, which seems more appropriate considering the cost and weight of these valuable spices.

f 19:40 This was the myrrh and aloes, which were embalming spices.

g 19:42 See Isaiah 53:9.

Twenty

The Empty Tomb

¹Very early Sunday morning,[h] before sunrise, Miriam Magdalene made her way to the tomb. And when she arrived she discovered that the stone that sealed the entrance to the tomb was moved away! ²So she went running as fast as she could to go tell Peter the Rock and the other disciple, the one Jesus loved.[i] She told them, "They've taken the Lord's body from the tomb, and we don't know where he is!"

³Then Peter the Rock and the other disciple jumped up and ran to the tomb to go see for themselves. ⁴They started out together, but the other disciple outran Peter and reached the tomb first.[j] ⁵He didn't enter the tomb, but peeked in, and saw only the linen cloths lying there. ⁶Then Peter came behind him and went right into the tomb. He too noticed the linen cloths lying there, ⁷but the burial cloth that had been on Jesus' head had been rolled up and placed separate from the other cloths.

⁸Then the other disciple who had reached the tomb first went in, and after one look, he believed![k] ⁹For until then they hadn't understood the Scriptures that prophesied[l] that he was destined to rise from the dead.[m] ¹⁰Puzzled, Peter the Rock and the other disciple then left and went back to their homes.

---

h 20:1 Or "On the first day of the week."

i 20:2 This was obviously John the apostle, the author of this gospel.

j How did John outrun Peter to the tomb? Love will always "outrun" curiosity. Some are simply curious to know Jesus, but we must be those who are passionate to experience his love and power.

k 20:8 It was lovers of Jesus that were the first to realize the resurrection of Christ. What did John see that caused him to believe? Perhaps it was the linen burial cloths that had not been unwrapped, but simply were empty. And the cloth that had been wrapped around his head was rolled up and placed aside. Jesus left everything pertaining to the old creation in the tomb, signified by the linen cloths and handkerchief left behind.

l 20:9 Some of these prophesies would include Psalm 2:6–8 and 16:10, Isaiah 53:10–12, Jonah 1:17 and Hosea 6:2.

m 20:9 As translated from the Aramaic.

[11]Miriam arrived *back at the tomb,* broken and sobbing. She stooped to peer inside, and through her tears [12]she saw two angels in dazzling white robes, sitting where Jesus' body had been laid—one at the head and one at the feet![a]

[13]"Dear woman, why are you crying?" they asked.

Miriam answered, "They have taken away my Lord, and I don't know where they've laid him."

[14]Then she turned around to leave, and there was Jesus standing in front of her, but she didn't realize that it was him!

[15]He said to her, **"Dear woman, why are you crying? Who are you looking for?"**

Miriam answered, thinking it was only the gardener, "Sir, if you have taken his body somewhere else, tell me, and I will go and . . ."

[16]**"Miriam,"** Jesus interrupted her.

Turning to face him, she said, "Rabboni!" (Aramaic for "my teacher")

[17]Jesus cautioned her, **"Miriam, don't hold on to me now, for I haven't yet ascended to God, my Father. And he's not only my Father and God, but now he's your Father and your God! Now go to my brothers[b] and tell them what I've told you, that 'I am ascending to my Father—and your Father, to my God—and your God!'"**

[18]Then Miriam Magdalene left to inform the disciples of her encounter with Jesus. "I have seen the Lord!" she told them. And she gave them his message.

Jesus Appears to His Disciples

[19]That evening,[c] the disciples gathered together. And because they were afraid of reprisals from the Jewish leaders, they had locked the doors to the place where they met. But suddenly Jesus appeared among them and

---

a 20:12 This becomes a picture of the two golden cherubim engraved on the mercy seat, peering down into the treasures of grace.

b 20:17 This is the first time in John's gospel that Jesus calls his disciples "brothers." See Hebrews 2:10–12.

c 20:19 Or "That Sunday evening."

said,[a] **"Peace to you!"**[b] [20]Then he showed them the wounds of his hands and his side—they were overjoyed to see the Lord with their own eyes!

[21]Jesus repeated his greeting, **"Peace to you!"** And he told them, **"Just as the Father has sent me, I'm now sending you."** [22]Then, taking a deep breath, he blew[c] on them and said, **"Receive the Holy Spirit.**[d] [23]**I send you to preach the forgiveness**[e] **of sins—and people's sins will be forgiven. But if you don't proclaim the forgiveness of their sins, they will remain guilty."**[f]

Jesus Appears to Thomas

[24]One of the twelve wasn't present when Jesus appeared to them—it was Thomas, whose nickname was "the Twin." [25]So the disciples informed him, "We have seen the Lord with our own eyes!"

Still unconvinced, Thomas replied, "There's no way I'm going to believe this unless I personally see the wounds of the nails[g] in his hands, touch them with my finger, and put my hand into the wound of his side where he was pierced!"

[26]Then eight days later, Thomas and all the others were in the house together. And even though all the doors were locked, Jesus suddenly stood before them! **"Peace to you,"** he said.

---

a 20:19 Or "came and stood among them."

b 20:19 This is the idiomatic equivalent of saying, "Hello, everyone!"

c 20:22 The Greek word used here does not appear elsewhere in the New Testament, however, it is the same word found in the Septuagint for God "breathed" into Adam's nostrils the breath of life (Genesis 2:7). The beginning of new creation life came from the breath of Jesus. The mighty wind of Acts is for power, the breath of Jesus breathed into his disciples in John 20:22 was for life.

d 20:22 Or "accept the Sacred Breath."

e 20:23 Or "removal, acquittal."

f 20:23 Or "If you forgive someone for their sins, their sins will be discharged, but if you retain their sins, their sins will be retained." Jesus was not giving absolute authority to forgive the guilt of sins, for God alone has that right (Mark 2:7), and the apostles at no time assumed that authority. What he gives them, in the context of being his sent ones, is the authority to proclaim the gospel to the nations. If they refuse to go and preach the good news, then people will have no opportunity to believe it. See Acts 10:43–44 and 13:38.

g 20:25 The Aramaic is, "the blossom of the nails." You can imagine a wide nail head that when struck with a heavy mallet, "blossomed" over the sacred palm of our Lord Jesus. The wound of the nail had imprinted his entire palm. His wounds are like beautiful flowers to the lovers of God.

²⁷Then, looking into Thomas' eyes, he said, **"Put your finger here in the wounds of my hands. Here—put your hand into my wounded side and see for yourself. Thomas, don't give in to your doubts any longer, just believe!"**

²⁸Then the words spilled out of his heart—"You are my Lord, and you are my God!"

²⁹Jesus responded, **"Thomas, now that you've seen me, you believe. But there are those who have never seen me with their eyes but have believed in me with their hearts, and they will be blessed even more!"**

³⁰Jesus went on to do many more miraculous signs in the presence of his disciples, which are not even included in this book. ³¹But all that is recorded here is so that you will fully believe[a] that Jesus is the Anointed One, the Son of God, and that through your faith in him you will experience eternal life[b] by the power of his name!

Twenty-one

Jesus Appears at the Lake of Galilee

¹Later, Jesus appeared once again to a group of his disciples by the Sea of Galilee.[c] ²It happened one day while Peter the Rock, Thomas (the Twin), Nathanael (from Cana in Galilee), Jacob, John,[d] and two other disciples were all together. ³Peter told them, "I'm going fishing." And they all replied,

---

a 20:31 Or "never stop believing."
b 20:31 As translated from the Aramaic.
c 21:1 Or "the Sea of Tiberias."
d 21:2 Or in place of Jacob (James) and John, "the sons of Zebedee."

"We'll go with you."[a] So they went out and fished through the night, but caught nothing.

⁴Then at dawn, Jesus was standing there on the shore, but the disciples didn't realize that it was him! ⁵He called out to them, saying, **"Hey guys! Did you catch any fish?"**[b]

"Not a thing," they replied.

⁶Jesus shouted to them, **"Throw your net over the starboard side, and you'll catch some!"** And so they did as he said, and they caught so many fish they couldn't even pull in the net!

⁷Then the disciple whom Jesus loved said to Peter the Rock, "It's the Lord!" When Peter heard him say that, he quickly wrapped his outer garment around him, and because he was athletic,[c] he dove right into the lake to go to Jesus! ⁸The other disciples then brought the boat to shore, dragging their catch of fish. They weren't far from land, only about a hundred meters. ⁹And when they got to shore, they noticed a charcoal fire with some roasted fish and bread.[d] ¹⁰Then Jesus said, **"Bring some of the fish you just caught."**

¹¹So Peter the Rock waded into the water and helped pull the net to shore. It was full of many large fish, exactly one hundred and fifty-three,[e] but even with so many fish, the net was not torn.

¹²**"Come, let's have some breakfast,"** Jesus said to them.

---

a 21:3 According to Luke 24:49, the disciples were told to wait in Jerusalem for the day they would be clothed with power. These seven apostles were not following what they had been told, and for this reason they caught nothing until Jesus joined them. He became the eighth man.

b 21:5 Or "Have you caught anything to eat?"

c 21:7 As translated from the Aramaic. The Greek is literally, "because he was naked." This is very strange and most expositors make quite a case for this not being the case, in spite of the Greek saying he was, indeed, naked. The problem is solved by the Aramaic, which says, "because Peter was athletic, he dove into the water." There is no mention of being "naked" in the Aramaic.

d 21:9 It was while standing next to a fire that Peter denied Christ; now standing next to a fire, Jesus will restore his beloved friend.

e 21:11 This speaks of the great redemption of Christ for all nations and all people. 153 large fish points to a mighty harvest from among the people groups of the world. This great catch of fish begins the process of inner healing for Peter and the guilt of his denial of Christ. Peter began to follow Jesus because of a great catch of fish (Luke 5:2-10), so Jesus now repeats that miracle, inviting Peter to begin to follow Jesus again.

And not one of the disciples needed to ask who it was, because every one of them knew it was the Lord. ¹³Then Jesus came close to them and served them the bread and the fish. ¹⁴This was the third time Jesus appeared to his disciples after his resurrection.

Jesus Restores Peter

¹⁵After they had breakfast, Jesus said to Peter the Rock, **"Simon, son of John,ᶠ do you burn with loveᵍ for me more than these?"ʰ**

Peter answered, "Yes, Lord! You know that I have great affection for you!"

"Then take care of my lambs,"ⁱ Jesus said.

¹⁶Jesus repeated his question the second time, **"Simon, son of John, do you burn with love for me?"**

Peter answered, "Yes, my Lord! You know that I have great affection for you!"

"Then take care of my sheep," Jesus said.

¹⁷Then Jesus asked him again, **"Peter, son of John, do you have great affection for me?"**

---

f 21:15 The Aramaic is, "son of the Dove." See also verses 16 and 17.

g 21:15 The Aramaic word for love is *hooba*, and is taken from a root word that means, "to set on fire." This was the word Jesus would have used to ask Peter, "Do you burn with love for me?" Our love for Jesus must be passionate and kindle a holy flame within our hearts. See Song of Songs 8:6–7.

h 21:15 As often is the case, Jesus' words have more than one meaning. "These" can refer to the fish they had just caught, for Peter was a fisherman and loved to fish. He may have been counting and sorting the fish when Jesus asked him that question. But "these" most likely refers to the other disciples. It was Peter's boast that he loved Jesus more than the others, and though everyone else would leave him, Peter never would. That boast proved empty, as within hours of making the claim, Peter denied he even knew Jesus three times. So Jesus asks Peter three times if he loved him. In essence, Jesus knew how to bring healing to Peter and remove the pain of his denial. Three times Peter denied Jesus, but three times he makes his confession of his deep love for Christ. By the third time, the "crowing rooster" inside Peter had been silenced, and now he was ready to be a shepherd for Jesus' flock.

i 21:15 The Aramaic is, "feed my rams (male lambs)." This may refer to the other disciples. In verse 16 the Aramaic is simply, "sheep." And in verse 17 in Aramaic, Jesus uses the third term, "ewes (female lambs)." Some see in these that Peter was symbolically given charge of three flocks: Jews, Samaritans, and Gentiles. Regardless, men and women need to be cared for and fed by the leadership of Christ's church among the nations.

Peter was saddened by being asked the third time[a] and said, "My Lord, you know everything. You know that I burn with love for you!"

Jesus replied, **"Then feed my lambs! ¹⁸Peter, listen, when you were younger you made your own choices[b]and you went where you pleased. But one day when you are old,[c] others will tie you up and escort you where you would not choose to go—and you will spread out your arms."[d]** ¹⁹(Jesus said this to Peter as a prophecy of what kind of death he would die, for the glory of God.) And then he said, **"Peter, follow me!"**

²⁰Then Peter the Rock turned and saw that the disciple whom Jesus loved was following them. (This was the disciple who sat close to Jesus at the Last Supper and had asked him, "Lord, who is the one that will betray you?") ²¹So when Peter saw him, he asked Jesus, "What's going to happen to him?"

²²Jesus replied, **"If I decide to let him live until I return, what concern is that of yours? You must still keep on following me!"**

²³So the rumor started to circulate among the believers that this disciple wasn't going to die. But Jesus never said that, he only said, **"If I let him live until I return, what concern is that of yours?"**

Conclusion

²⁴I, John,[e] am that disciple who has written these things to testify of the truth, and we[f] know that what I've documented is accurate. ²⁵Jesus did

---

a 21:17 Three times Peter denied Christ, so Jesus gave him three opportunities to redeem himself.

b 21:18 Or "you girded yourself."

c 21:18 The Aramaic is, "greyheaded."

d 21:18 Or "stretch out your hands." This was clearly a hint of the martyrdom Peter would experience in Rome one day, where historians have recorded that Peter was crucified upside down, at his request, because he said that he was unworthy to be crucified in the same way as his Lord. He once said he was willing to die for our Lord Jesus; now Christ promises that will happen.

e 21:24 The evidence both internally and externally clearly points to John as the author of this book, thus the explicit reference here.

f 21:24 The word "we" implies that John had conferred with the other disciples, as he has left us an accurate account of the life of Jesus Christ.

countless things that I haven't included here. And if every one of his works were written down *and described one by one,*[a] I suppose that the world itself wouldn't have enough room to contain the books that would have to be written![b]

---

a 21:25 Implied in the Aramaic.

b 21:25 The Aramaic is very poetic, "The world itself would be emptied out into the books that would be written." An alternate translation of the Aramaic could read, "I suppose that forever is still not enough time for all the books to be written!"

About the Translator

Dr. Brian Simmons is known as a passionate lover of God. After a dramatic conversion to Christ, Brian knew that God was calling him to go to the unreached people of the world and present the gospel of God's grace to all who would listen. With his wife Candice and their three children, he spent nearly eight years in the tropical rain forest of the Darien Province of Panama as a church planter, translator, and consultant. Brian was involved in the Paya-Kuna New Testament translation project. He studied linguistics and Bible translation principles with New Tribes Mission. After their ministry in the jungle, Brian was instrumental in planting a thriving church in New England (U.S.), and now travels full time as a speaker and Bible teacher. He has been happily married to Candice for over forty-two years and is known to boast regularly of his children and grandchildren. Brian and Candice may be contacted at:

brian@passiontranslation.com

Facebook.com/passiontranslation

Twitter.com/tPtBible

For more information about the translation project or any of Brian's books, please visit:

thePassionTranslation.com

stairwayministries.org

thePassionTranslation.com